# THE STRUGGLE OF PRAYER

OTHER BOOKS BY DONALD G. BLOESCH

*Centers of Christian Renewal*
*The Christian Life and Salvation*
*The Crisis of Piety*
*The Christian Witness in a Secular Age*
*Christian Spirituality East and West* (coauthor)
*The Reform of the Church*
*The Ground of Certainty*
*Servants of Christ* (editor)
*The Evangelical Renaissance*
*Wellsprings of Renewal*
*Light a Fire*
*The Invaded Church*
*Jesus Is Victor!: Karl Barth's Doctrine of Salvation*
*The Orthodox Evangelicals* (coeditor)
*Essentials of Evangelical Theology:*
*God, Authority, and Salvation* (Vol. I)
*Essentials of Evangelical Theology: Life, Ministry, and Hope* (Vol. II)

# The Struggle of Prayer

*Donald G. Bloesch*

HARPER & ROW, PUBLISHERS

SAN FRANCISCO

Cambridge
Hagerstown
Philadelphia
New York

*1817*

London
Mexico City
São Paulo
Sydney

Dedicated to the memory
of the Puritan father,
Richard Sibbes

FIRST EDITION

*Designed by Jim Mennick*

---

**Library of Congress Cataloging in Publication Data**

Bloesch, Donald G        1928–
THE STRUGGLE OF PRAYER.

Includes index
1. Prayer.   I. Title.
BV210.2.B576      248.3′2      79–3589
ISBN 0–06–060797–1

---

80   81   82   83   84   10   9   8   7   6   5   4   3   2   1

# Contents

# Preface

*Thesis*

I have written this book on prayer in order to delineate the outlines of an evangelical spirituality. Prayer is the heart of spirituality and therefore has a certain priority over other areas of the spiritual life. My focus of attention is on Christian prayer, but it is well to note that prayer is a universal phenomenon, firmly rooted in the human condition. Barth aptly calls prayer our "incurable God-sickness."

In this work I shall explore the differences and convergences between two types of spirituality: mysticism and biblical personalism. I am therefore continuing a discussion already begun in two earlier books of mine: *The Crisis of Piety* and *The Ground of Certainty*. I aim not for a rapprochement between prophetic religion and mysticism but for a clarification of the issues that divide and unite these two spiritual outlooks. While acknowledging the mystical dimension in true prayer, I basically stand in the tradition of the biblical prophets and the Protestant Reformation, which sees prayer not as *recitation* (as in formalistic religion) or *meditation* (as in mysticism) but as *dialogue* between a living God and the one who has been touched by his grace.

True prayer is here understood as God reaching out to humanity and calling for a response of obedience, not as humanity rising to God in order to become one with him (the mystical ideal). This is not to deny that a primary aim of prayer is to be conformed to the will of God; however, this should be seen not as deification or divinization but as the realization of true humanity made possible only by the outpouring of unmerited grace.

So much mysticism begins in mist and ends in heresy. But there is another kind of mysticism, one purified and corrected by the biblical evangel. This kind of mysticism is an integral dimension of the prophetic prayer of biblical faith. Mystical awareness needs to be united with a fervent belief in the biblical message. Mystical experience needs to be transformed and redirected by faith in the crucified and risen Savior.

My second reason for writing this book is to counteract the current misunderstandings of prayer, as in pop mysticism and cultic evangelicalism, where prayer is reduced to a consciousness-raising experience or a therapeutic technique. I have also sought to combat the ritual prayer that is so prevalent in mainline Protestantism and Catholicism, though I do not discount the proper place for liturgical forms in public worship.

I freely acknowledge my indebtedness to three great warriors of prayer: Martin Luther, the father of modern evangelicalism, whose biblical fidelity and catholicity are being rediscovered by Roman Catholic scholars; Richard Sibbes, noted Puritan preacher in late sixteenth- and early seventeenth-century England; and Peter Taylor Forsyth, British Congregationalist minister and theologian and modern heir of the Puritans (d. 1921). All three men gave due recognition to the dimension of importunity in prayer, which has been sorely neglected in Protestant spirituality since Schleiermacher and Troeltsch. These evangelical luminaries rightly saw that prayer is an act of the will and not simply resting in the stillness. While acknowledging that God gives many unasked-for gifts, they also insisted that great gifts are always given in response to great prayer. Yet they did not deny the mystical element in prayer and frequently alluded to the rapture that accompanies the union with Christ realized in faith. Moreover, they shared a high view of the church and the sacraments and were firm advocates of Christian unity. Richard Sibbes occasionally cited Luther in his writings, and

Forsyth clearly reveals his dependence on both the mainline Reformers as well as on the whole Puritan tradition. Whereas Calvin was more likely to stress submission to the will of God without denying the dimension of importunity, these men emphasized the need to strive with God in prayer; Luther and Sibbes could even speak of prayer as "conquering God" insofar as it sought to bind God to his own promises. The sometimes extravagant claims that Luther and Sibbes made concerning the power of prayer need to be held in tension with Calvin's perception that God remains sovereign even in the life of prayer.

The saints of evangelical faith, including Luther, Calvin, Kierkegaard, Forsyth, and many others, recognize that people turn to God in the anguish of their spirit (cf. Job 7:11) and find a God who will not let them alone (cf. Job 7:17–20; 9:14, 32). They encourage us never to lose heart but to persist in praying, wishing and seeking until the awaited liberation appears, even though it may well be in a form that we did not at first anticipate. From the great saints of evangelicalism we can learn to face the future with hope and confidence because prayer is "our power and victory in every trial" (Luther).

This book is intended as a theology of prayer and not as a practical guide for the development of the life of prayer. At the same time, I hope that those who read it will benefit not just in an intellectual but also in a practical way. I would indeed be grateful if it encouraged some to move from the prayer of rote to the prayer of the heart, which is prayer with "faith, fervency, constancy and feeling" (Sibbes). I write as only a learner in the life of prayer, not as an expert, and I look forward to an interchange of my ideas on this subject with those of the readers.

# Acknowledgments

This is to acknowledge the substantial assistance that I have received from my wife, Brenda, who has been a copy editor of several of my recent books. I have also profited from the insights and comments of Dr. Charles Whiston, director of the National Prayer Tryst Fellowship, of which I was a member; Father Benedict Viviano of the Aquinas Institute of Theology; Dr. Rudolf Schade of Elmhurst College, and Mr. Lance Wonders, pastor of the First Presbyterian church, Andrew, Iowa. I am also very grateful to Miss Lillian Staiger of the Dubuque Theological Seminary library for her aid in procuring needed books.

I wish to thank *The Reformed Journal* for granting permission for the republication in revised form of the article "Prayer and Mysticism," which appeared in the March and April (1976) issues of that magazine. This article was originally my presidential address to the members of the American Theological Society, Midwest Division, at Elmhurst College, Elmhurst, Illinois in April 1975.

Some of these chapters were presented in embryonic form in lectures at various churches and colleges during the past several years.

# Abbreviations

Scripture references are from the Revised Standard Version, unless otherwise indicated by the following abbreviations:

New International Version     NIV
King James Version     KJV
New English Bible     NEB
Good News Bible     GNB
New American Standard Bible     NASB
Living Bible     LB

I appeal to you, brethren . . . to strive together with me in your prayers to God on my behalf.

ROMANS 15:30

Nor is prayer ever heard more abundantly than in such agony and groanings of a struggling faith.

MARTIN LUTHER

Praying is a kind of wrestling and contending with God, a striving with him.

RICHARD SIBBES

True prayer is a struggle with God, in which one triumphs through the triumph of God.

SØREN KIERKEGAARD

To feed the soul we must toil at prayer. . . . It is the assimilation of a holy God's moral strength.

P. T. FORSYTH

# I

# Introduction

In a time of renewed interest in mysticism and spirituality, it is appropriate to explore the meaning of biblical prayer. For many people today, tantalized by the new fashions in theology and religion, prayer is an experience of self-awareness by which one enters into the inner sanctum of the soul. Or it is a tried and tested means of ecstatic release from the stress of daily living. Or it is a highly refined technique designed to prepare oneself for union with the ground of all being. That prayer in the biblical perspective is radically different from the foregoing conceptions will become readily apparent.

The question that needs to be pondered is whether the pop mysticism that presently dominates the spiritual scene is in accord with the mystical heritage of the Christian faith. The renowned Catholic historian of religions R. C. Zaehner answers with a redoubtable no, maintaining that mysticism in the Christian sense is qualitatively different from mysticism in general.[1] This allegation is open to question, however, in light of the many scholars of religion who detect certain universal motifs at work in every variety of mysticism.[2]

It has been customary in Protestant circles to draw a sharp distinction between the faith of the biblical prophets and evangelical Reformers and the religion of the mystics. Because this distinction is vigorously contested especially by Catholic scholars, it is well to reexamine the complex relationship between mystical spirituality and evangelical piety. It is becoming generally recognized that the Reformers themselves were deeply influenced by Catholic mysticism, and this is even more true of the spiritual movements of purification after the Reformation, Pietism and Puritanism. The biblical roots of many of the mystics are now being rediscovered, and the hope is dawning that the historic barriers between these two spiritual traditions might at last be overcome.

In the context of this study, *mysticism* refers to a type of religion characterized by an immediate or direct perception of the presence of God and an attempt to actualize union with divinity. *Evangelicalism,* by contrast, signifies a type of religion where the knowledge of God is mediated through a particular historical witness to divine revelation and where the accent is placed on the service of God's glory rather than elevation into glory. The appeal in mysticism is to an experience that transcends the subject-object polarity, whereas the appeal in evangelicalism is to a definitive revelation in history attested and recorded in the Bible. Christian mystics seek to interpret the experience of unity or oneness with God in Christian terms, but the basic orientation is still ahistorical where devotion to Jesus is only a means to union with the eternal ground of all things.

This book attempts to open up a dialogue between the evangelical and mystical traditions. My purpose, however, is not to reconcile evangelical spirituality with mysticism but instead to make it possible for evangelicals to appreciate some of the great mystics who, for the most part, remained faithful to biblical truth despite their dependence on an alien philosophy, such as Neo-Platonism. Bengt Hoffman has made a signal contribution in his *Luther and the Mystics* by revealing the mystical roots of Luther's faith, but he does not do justice to the originality of Luther's theology, particularly his doctrine of forensic justification, which sharply separates him from his mystical forebears.[3] Steven Ozment, in his *Homo Spiritualis,* argues convincingly that Luther and the mystics were definitely *not* saying the same thing in different ways.⁴ Yet it seems that Ozment too easily disregards the mystical themes in Luther's theology and ends by making Luther a purely ethical thinker concerned with humanization rather than with personal transfiguration in the image of Christ. It is my contention that Luther's spirituality was fundamentally different from that of the mystics, but this does not mean that he did not draw on his mystical heritage, in both negative and positive ways, in giving shape to his spirituality.

A book that has had a decisive influence on my understanding of prayer is Friedrich Heiler's *Prayer,* a study in the history and psychology of religion.⁵ Heiler, a convert from Roman Catholicism to Lutheranism, distinguishes between several different types of prayer, including the mystical and the prophetic.

In Heiler's schema, the first type, primitive prayer, characterizes animistic or tribal religion. Here prayer is largely spontaneous but at the same time egocentric, since the petitioner primarily seeks divine aid to ensure his or her own prosperity and protection. The motivation is twofold: self-gain and fear. Primitive people seek deliverance not from sin but from misfortune and danger. Their god is decidedly anthropomorphic, not almighty but often personable and sometimes arbitrary. An appeal to the sympathy or vanity of the god or gods is a recurring element in primitive prayer.

The second type of prayer, which signifies a higher level of civilization, is ritual prayer. Here prayer's efficacy is bound to the recitation of an exact formula, verbally precise and clearly articulated. Sacrifice is the crucial element in the religious life, and the prayer of thanksgiving fades into the background. An invocation of one or more higher beings frequently introduces ritual prayer. The content is the same as that of primitive prayer—petition for earthly blessings.

Among the ancient Greeks, we see primitive religion ethically deepened and aesthetically clarified. Petition for moral values is now regarded as central in prayer. But the Greeks knew nothing of the deep awareness of moral failure and sinfulness that led the saints of Christian faith to sigh for grace and forgiveness.

Greek religion was a natural religion tied very closely to Greek culture.

With the great philosophers (Heiler gives special attention to classical and Enlightenment thinkers) prayer becomes reflection on the highest good or resignation to the supreme order of things. The only petition deemed worthy of the philosopher is the prayer for the realization of moral values in the individual life. There is no longer a realistic communion with a living God, as in primitive prayer, but now only reverence for Nature or the ground of Nature. Heiler astutely shows that "rational philosophical thought means the disintegration and dissolution of prayer."[6]

The two highest types of prayer, in Heiler's typology, are mystical and prophetic prayer, and here we see the relevance of Heiler for our discussion. In mysticism God is an "Eternal Rest" or "perfect Ideal," not living, active Will, as in biblical religion. The goal in mystical prayer is to become one with the Infinite. The emphasis is on love toward God and union with God. Formal prayer is seen as a preliminary stage to interior prayer, which consists in meditation and contemplation. For the mystic, prayer is a technique that facilitates union with the Eternal. Petitions for the necessities of life are considered carnal, since worldly needs are not that important and one should not seek to satisfy them. Heiler, who is speaking of Christian as well as non-Christian mysticism, sees Christian mysticism as a combination of Neo-Platonism and biblical piety, with the former predominating.

Prophetic prayer, exemplified in the biblical prophets and rediscovered by the Protestant Reformers, is essentially a spontaneous outburst of emotion. Its chief content is the utterance of need. The worshipper seeks not ecstatic union with God but only to feel his presence in blessed, living communion with him. Faith toward God and love for neighbor are emphasized over unitive love with God. Not withdrawal from the world but the transformation of the world into the kingdom of God is the goal of prophetic religion. Heiler includes in this category the leading prophetic figures of Judaism and Islam as well as Christianity, since the former are also religions of revelation.

Heiler's analysis has often been subject to severe criticism, especially by Roman Catholic and Anglican scholars who are concerned with defending the biblical foundations of Christian mysticism. Louis Bouyer claims that Heiler fails to perceive that prophetic religion can too easily become utilitarian; it seems that we seek God only for his gifts and not for himself.[7] Some have charged that Heiler does not do justice to the missionary zeal of many of the Catholic mystics, for he maintains that mystics seek exclusive solitude and lack missionary motivation.[8] In defense of Heiler, it should be said that he is working with ideal types and freely admits that some of his examples only partially reflect the category in which they are placed. He is willing to recognize that "many Christian mystics . . . influenced by the spirit of prayer of the scriptures express themselves naively in worship." In this context, he mentions Teresa of Avila, who "was accustomed in her 'prayer of quiet' to place her needs quite simply before God."[9]

It should also be remembered that Heiler is working in the area of the phenomenology of religion. Any one of these various forms of prayer, empirically considered, can become idolatrous and demonic, and any one can be transformed into genuine prayer from the theological perspective. Yet none of these phenomenological types of prayer can become genuine Christian prayer apart from conscious surrender to and union with the living Christ; all these forms of prayer fall short of true prayer when the Holy Spirit is absent.

In this book, I shall be working primarily with two categories: biblical, evangelical prayer and mystical prayer. My understanding of the first is roughly equivalent to Heiler's prophetic prayer, except that I seek to base it more fully on Scripture rather than on an empirical analysis of religion. In Chapter 6, I spell out at length the essential differences as well as the convergences between these two types of prayer and spirituality. I shall also be making some important distinctions between biblical and formalistic (or ritual) prayer.

One type of prayer that Heiler did not consider, undoubtedly because of its fairly recent appearance on the religious scene, is secular, political prayer. Here prayer is "not a conversation with God but a conversation with the world."[10] It is neither the pouring out of the soul (as in biblical prayer) nor contemplative adoration (as in mysticism) but reflection on the needs of the world and then acting to meet these needs. It is not withdrawal from the world but penetration through the world to God (J. A. T. Robinson). In this respect it might be described as a type of secular mysticism.[11]

As I appraise the various types of prayer, as outlined by Heiler, I see the danger in moralism as well as in mysticism. Prophetic prayer can degenerate into a purely ethical religion if it is separated from its spiritual and mystical roots. Prayer is not simply a discourse directed to God nor is it exclusively a verbal operation (as Heiler readily acknowledges). Its source and mainspring is the Holy Spirit, who transcends all verbalizing and conceptualizing. Unless he intercedes, our prayer is not true prayer. Yet we must insist against the radical mystics that the Holy Spirit does not transcend rationality.

I agree with the prophets and the Reformers that the essence of prayer is not a mystical lifting up of the mind to God but the descent of the Spirit into our hearts (cf. Isa. 45:8; 64:1; Pss. 42:8; 144:5–7; Ezek. 2:1, 2; Zech. 12:10). It is not climbing the mystical ladder to heaven but taking hold of the outstretched hand of God (cf. Isa. 64:7). The Reformers remind us that we of ourselves cannot lift ourselves into the presence of God. We must wait for God to come to us, and he has done so in the person of his Son, Jesus Christ. Our petition is a response to the initiative of God; our justification and sanctification are fruits of our election by God.

That effectual prayer—and, indeed, Christian life itself—are conditional on the outpouring of divine grace is powerfully attested in these words from a recent Catholic hymn:

> Word of God, come down on earth,
>   Living rain from heav'n descending;
> Touch our hearts and bring to birth
>   Faith and hope and love unending.
> Word almighty, we revere you;
>   Word made flesh, we long to hear you.[12]

The distinction between biblical, evangelical prayer and mystical prayer does not necessarily correspond to that between Protestantism and Roman Catholicism. There have been many Protestant mystics, and there have been some vehement critics of mysticism among Roman Catholic scholars.[13] Some Catholic theologians (such as the Dominican P. Festugière) even accept the validity of the kind of distinction that Heiler makes between prophetic and mystical prayer. This can safely be said: Just as Roman Catholicism has been too ready to assimilate mysticism uncritically, so Reformed Protestantism has been too quick to deny its universally true and abiding insights.[14]

While biblical, evangelical prayer converges at some points with mystical prayer, especially as found among the great Christian mystics, it differs radically from the ritual prayer that dominates even a religion such as Islam[15] and from the philosophic prayer that has characterized the great schools of antiquity as well as modern forms of philosophy. Whereas the Stoics recognized praise and the summoning of the soul to acquiescense in God's will but not petition, biblical religion even allows for petitions for benefits and virtues. Solomon besought the Lord for virtue (1 Kings 3:9) and for benefits (8:22–53).

The biblical Christian can only pray empty-handed, as the thirteenth-century Dominican preacher William Peraldus expressed it. Or, as Augustine observed, "The best disposition for praying is that of being desolate, forsaken, stripped of everything."[16] Unlike the ritualist, we know that any sacrifice we bring before God is stained by sin and therefore unworthy of acceptance apart from the mediation and intercession of Jesus Christ. Our hope depends not on the right technique or the proper phrase or gesture, which borders on magic, but on the promises of God to look with favor on those who throw themselves on his mercy and who acknowledge the efficacy of the atoning sacrifice of his Son, Jesus Christ, for their redemption.

As I see it, true prayer is neither mystical rapture nor ritual observance nor philosophical reflection: it is the outpouring of the soul before a living God, the crying to God "out of the depths." Such prayer can only be uttered by one convicted of sin by the grace of God and moved to confession by the Spirit of God. True prayer is an encounter with the Holy in which we realize not only our creatureliness and guilt but also the joy of knowing that our sins are forgiven through the atoning death of the divine savior, Jesus Christ. In such an encounter, we are impelled not only to bow before God and seek his mercy but also to offer thanksgiving for grace that goes out to undeserving sinners.

## NOTES

1. R. C. Zaehner, *Mysticism: Sacred and Profane* (Oxford: Clarendon Press, 1957).
2. See Sidney Spencer, *Mysticism in World Religion* (Baltimore: Penguin Books, 1963); F. C. Happold, *Mysticism: A Study and an Anthology* (Baltimore: Penguin Books, 1963); and Geoffrey Parrinder, *Mysticism in the World's Religions* (New York: Oxford University Press, 1977).
3. Bengt R. Hoffman, *Luther and the Mystics* (Minneapolis: Augsburg, 1976). Hoffman can be criticized for not giving adequate recognition to the tension between Luther's evangelical piety and mystical spirituality.
4. Steven E. Ozment, *Homo Spiritualis* (Leiden: Brill, 1969).
5. Friedrich Heiler, *Prayer,* trans. and ed. Samuel McComb (New York: Oxford University Press, 1958).
6. Heiler, *Prayer,* p. 102.
7. Louis Bouyer, *The Meaning of Sacred Scripture,* trans. Mary Perkins Ryan (Notre Dame, Ind.: University of Notre Dame Press, 1958), pp. 135–137. Also see his *Introduction to Spirituality,* trans. Mary Perkins Ryan (New York: Desclee, 1963, 2nd printing), pp. 289 ff.; and A. Léonard, "Studies on

the Phenomena of Mystical Experience," in A. Plé et al., eds., *Mystery and Mysticism* (New York: Philosophical Library, 1956), pp. 70 ff.

8. See Robert L. Simpson, *The Interpretation of Prayer in the Early Church* (Philadelphia: Westminster Press, 1965), p. 112. It seems that Heiler is especially vulnerable on this point, since he does not consider that some Roman Catholic religious orders, which draw on the mystical heritage of the faith, are conspicuous for their missionary outreach. Nor does he appear to recognize that Protestant Pietism, which united mystical themes with Reformation piety, was responsible for the outpouring of evangelical missions. Nonetheless it can be argued that mystical motifs were definitely subordinated to practical concerns in Pietism: its asceticism was innerworldly, not otherworldly. According to Troeltsch, Pietism represents the sect-ideal within the church, not the mystical ideal (in his *The Social Teachings of the Christian Churches,* trans. Olive Wyon [London: Allen & Unwin, 1950, 3rd impression], Vol. 2, p. 717). The mystical ideal is more truly exemplified in Valentin Weigel and Sebastian Franck of the radical Reformation, who were indifferent to missions.

A case could also be made that the Catholic orders, including many of the contemplative ones, derive their missionary concern from the demands of the gospel and not from Neo-Platonic mysticism. It is true that exclusively mystical societies like the Friends of God (fourteenth century), the Quietists, the spiritualistic Quakers (as opposed to the evangelical Quakers), the Philadelphians (seventeenth century), the Rosicrucians, the Theosophists, and the Infinite Way movement of Joel Goldsmith are not noted for a passion to convert the masses; their motivation is simply a desire to impart secrets of the higher life to kindred spiritual souls. Troeltsch points out that mysticism "leads to the formation of groups on a purely personal basis, with no permanent form, which also tend to weaken the significance of forms of worship, doctrine and the historical element" (*Social Teachings,* Vol. 2, p. 993). The purpose of the mystical society is to share personal experiences and to cultivate individual spirituality, not to uphold an authoritative Word from God or herald an exclusive message apart from which there is no salvation. The concern in pure mysticism is the quest for enlightenment, not the witness to a definitive historical revelation.

9. Heiler, *Prayer,* p. 240.

10. Douglas Rhymes, *Prayer in the Secular City* (Philadelphia: Westminster Press, 1967), p. 48.

11. Mysticism is now being rediscovered by theologians who have been associated with secular and political theology. See Dorothee Sölle, *Death by Bread Alone,* trans. David L. Scheidt (Philadelphia: Fortress Press, 1978).

12. James Quinn, S.J. From *New Hymns for All Seasons* (London: Chapman, 1972), p. 25 (no. 10). Reprinted in *Catholic Book of Worship* (Ottawa, Canada: Canadian Catholic Conference, 1972, No. 364).

13. Among Catholic critics of a purely mystical religion are Hans Küng, Thomas Molnar, P. Festugière, Matthew Fox, Simon Tugwell, and Hans Urs von Balthasar.

14. Those who stand in the Reformed tradition will acknowledge that a Christian can at the same time be a mystic, but they will insist that this means a radically qualified mysticism, qualified by faith in the self-revelation of a divine mediator in human history.
15. For most Moslems, prayer is valueless unless offered in a state of ritual purity. Moreover, in order to be effective, the prayer must be said in Arabic.
16. Cited in Jacques Ellul, *Prayer and Modern Man,* trans. C. Edward Hopkin (New York: Seabury Press, 1970), p. 105.

# The Crisis of Prayer

## THE NEW RELIGIOUS SITUATION

There can be no doubt that authentic biblical, evangelical prayer is now in eclipse. Despite the resurgence of evangelicalism in this country in particular, what has often resulted is a hybrid religion in which the Christian faith is combined with purely cultural values. Too often a vague religiosity has supplanted biblical piety, and this means that secularism is still triumphant, though it appears in a new guise. The opening to the East has abetted the trend toward experientialism and mysticism, and consequently prayer itself has come to be conceived in a new way. No longer petition to a personal God and intercession on behalf of the world, prayer is now an experience of spirituality, entering into the depth dimension of existence.

The disciplines of devotion have receded into the background as people seek instant salvation through prescribed and easily-learned techniques. The often painful and laborious struggle to attain spiritual maturity in Christ that characterized the great saints of the past (both Catholic and Protestant) is singularly absent from the current fascination with spirituality.

Walter Wagoner's indictment of the prayer life of theological students several years ago is still valid today:

> Students suffer from the general syndrome of Protestant churches: they've become artful dodgers of a disciplined prayer life. They use

social action, spiritual guruism—in the form of psychological counseling—and a scrupulously academic approach to the study of religion as a substitute to evade the problem of a totally religious
prayer.[1]

While biblical, prophetic prayer is being partly rediscovered
in some of the subcultures of our time, such as the small evangelical sects and Jesus people, the mainstream of American culture is becoming increasingly removed from the naiveté of New
Testament religion. The growing liturgical worship in the mainline churches more often than not signifies a formalizing of the
prayer life that spells the death of a realistic communion with a
living God. Religion becomes relegated to the private sphere of
life, so that it is possible to cultivate an interior religion but remain silent on the grave ethical issues that confront humankind
today, including indiscriminate abortion, nuclear stockpiling,
euthanasia, and crimes against nature and the animal creation.
Charles Fager has aptly observed, "We live in a nation that is
not merely secular, in the sense of being emancipated from religious frames of reference, but is even actively pagan, that is to
say contemptuous of and even hostile toward the values these
traditions represent."[2]

On the European scene, secularism manifests itself in a more
aggressive atheism that seeks to stifle the religious spirit. Social-
istic welfare states, instead of freeing people to give time and
energy to the work of the church, tend to foster a servile dependence on the state, thus making the church appear anachronis-
tic. The startling drop in church attendance in both nominally
Catholic and Protestant countries attests to the emergence of a
secularistic mentality that celebrates emancipation from the religious and moral taboos of the past. Less than 6 percent of the
total population attend church regularly in England and less
than 3 percent in West Germany and Scandinavia. Well-organ-
ized radical groups in several of these countries are pushing for
the abolition of laws against incest and for the lowering of the
legal age for homosexual relations. In France, the intelligentsia

has largely been lost to Marxism and atheistic existentialism, and Marxist philosophy has increasingly made inroads in the working class.[3] No wonder that French Cardinal Suhard has described his nation as a new mission field. In Italy, once the center of Christian civilization, atheistic secularism now commands the loyalties of an ever growing number of people, especially of college-educated youth. One observer comments:

> Nowhere have I ever sensed the death of God so strongly as I did at an early evening mass in the cathedral of St. Mark in Venice. Tourists were milling about in the twilight, looking up at mosaics and then down at their guidebooks. Only a handful of nuns and elderly women were gathered in the pews, appearing more like Greek fates than worshipers of a Risen Lord.[4]

In many European nations, the churches are seen more as custodians of the values of a religiocultural heritage or as welfare organizations rather than communities of faith in a supernatural redemption. No longer "a Divine Society" on earth, the church has increasingly assumed the image of "a purely human institution" with a dual function—"that of providing certain unnecessary but pleasing ceremonies to mark the turning-points in domestic and national life; and that of serving humanitarian ends in relation to the sick and needy at home and abroad."[5]

The steady erosion of Christian belief in the European countries is, not surprisingly, reflected in the abandonment of biblical prayer. R. Gregor Smith maintains: "It is probably not an exaggeration to say that the vast mass of even conscientious church members have entirely relinquished the habit of private prayer in any of the conventional forms."[6] Similarly, Jacques Ellul concludes that there is a "drying up of private prayer. People read the Bible less, meditate less, and pray individually less and less."[7] Helmut Thielicke gives an even more dour picture: "The time when prayer meant knocking on a door that would then open . . . has gone. The hour has come when God is a door that is permanently closed, when transcendence is silent, when the empirical consciousness posits its own frequencies as absolute."[8]

This is not to deny that even in the secularized European nations, including those behind the Iron Curtain, biblical religion and ipso facto biblical prayer survive and in some communities even flourish. What I am suggesting is that in the power centers of the culture, including the professional-managerial class and the universities, aggressive secularism is on the rise and Christianity as an intellectual option is summarily dismissed. This is increasingly true on the American scene as well. The eminent sociologist Peter Berger predicts that by the twenty-first century, religious believers are likely to be found only in small enclaves, huddled together to resist a worldwide secular culture.[9]

It should be acknowledged that even the experts have been confounded by the surprising work of the Holy Spirit and that in past history even the most entrenched bastions of infidelity have not been able to withstand the transforming impact of the gospel. Revival of true religion is still possible even in the encroaching desert of secularism, but what we are experiencing now especially on the American scene is little more than a revival of interest in religion. That we are living in a new religious situation, one that is increasingly removed from the historic Christian faith, is nowhere better attested than in the reinterpretation of the meaning of prayer.

## THE MISUNDERSTANDING OF PRAYER

There are probably as many misunderstandings of prayer as there are misconceptions of God. In a time when new religions are emerging to fill the metaphysical vacuum engendered by secularism, it is not surprising that prayer and the whole of spirituality are being drastically reinterpreted.

In popular folk piety, prayer is often understood as a form of self-therapy, as a technique to attain self-identity or self-fulfillment. It is commonly held that the true answer to prayer does not come from an outside power but resides in the act itself. In the New Thought movement, "every self-treatment for more life, health, and goodness is prayer."[10]

Magical practices are rampant in folk religion, and here we see an affinity with the primitive religion of animism. Mantras, popularized in Transcendental Meditation, are none other than magical devices whereby the repetition of certain key words or phrases is believed to have automatic efficacy. In the Local Church sect of Witness Lee, the repetition of the phrase, "Lord Jesus" is considered necessary to gain the desired result.

The influence of American pragmatic philosophy is conspicuous in the neotranscendentalist and positive thinking movements. Prayer is deemed beneficial because it is shown to work in actual life and practice. This is also true for sections of the charismatic movement. Merlin Carothers, for example, commends the prayer of praise because signs and wonders follow upon such prayer.[11]

In some popular evangelical and charismatic circles, prayer is seen as a human technique for bending the will of God. It is a demand for results, not conformity to the will of God. Many charismatics are accustomed to speak of getting hold of spirit power (cf. manna in primitive religion). The theologically appropriate expression is to let the Holy Spirit in his power get hold of me. Prayer chains, which are increasingly in vogue in some of these circles, reduce prayer to magic; here again prayer is viewed as an attempt to control or channel divine power.[12]

Monistic mysticism, which gained ascendancy already in the nineteenth century, the Age of Romanticism, reconceives God as the ground of nature or the abysmal depth of being, and prayer too is given a new meaning and purpose. For Schleiermacher, prayer is only gratitude and resignation. It is getting in tune with the Infinite rather than earnest supplication to a personal God. It is withdrawal from the world and entrance into that deeper inner stillness where the union with God occurs. In a similar vein, Gerald Heard and Aldous Huxley see prayer as a means of breaking through the illusory world of sense into a sphere of timeless spiritual reality.

This same mood is apparent in the transcendentalist and neo-transcendentalist movements as well as in occultism. For Ralph Waldo Emerson, prayer is soliloquy, the contemplation of one's own inner being and the wonder of nature. In the theology of Mary Baker Eddy, the only true prayer is "the affirmation of Principle Allness." "Don't plead with God," she advised, "God is not influenced by man."[13] According to Glenn Clark, the founder of Camps Farthest Out, we should pray only for spiritual things, not material things. Annie Besant, one of the luminaries of the Theosophical movement, redefined prayer as "concentrated thought."[14] Similarly, in our day John Macquarrie defines prayer as a kind of thinking, especially *"compassionate thinking."*[15]

In existentialism, the one who prays does not speak or listen to God but instead comes to a new self-understanding. For Gregory Baum, prayer is no longer communication with divine reality; instead, "to pray is to be in touch with oneself in a new way."[16] Similarly, in Matthew Fox's theology "prayer is not talking to God" but is "a radical response to life," a process of rerooting oneself.[17] Michael Novak understands prayer as a form of intensified self-knowledge, "an attitude of radical openness."[18] At the Ecumenical Institute in Chicago, heavily influenced by existentialist philosophy, prayer is "a mechanism by which I articulate my problems to myself." According to Catholic theologian Don Brophy, "A person being completely open with another" is a form of prayer.[19]

In Paul Tillich, we see an attempt to combine existentialism and Christian mysticism, but the result is the loss of prayer in the realistic or biblical sense. For him, prayer is essentially meditation on the ground of being. Asked by one of his students if he prayed, he paused and then replied, "I meditate."[20] Tillich makes a place for supplication in the sense of bringing our needs and hopes into "the Spiritual Presence."[21] It is an act of elevating the mind, not conversation with a personal Being who stands over against humanity. In "spiritual prayer," the subject-object schema is transcended. Tillich's position parallels that of

Karl Jaspers, for whom the aim of philosophical contemplation "is no longer to achieve practical mundane results, but inward transfiguration."[22]

Secular and political theology reconceives prayer in terms of ethical engagement rather than petition and intercession (as in prophetic prayer) or spiritual ascent to the Godhead (as in mysticism). For Paul van Buren, prayer is reflection on the needs of one's neighbor and then acting to meet these needs. J. A. T. Robinson understands prayer as "opening oneself to the claim of the unconditional as it meets one in all the relationships of life."[23] As a result, "prayer and ethics are simply the inside and outside of the same thing."[24] Douglas Rhymes makes clear in his *Prayer in the Secular City* that prayer is man reflecting on himself and his world for the purpose of a deeper involvement in his world. It is "living . . . with a conscious motivation and purpose."[25] Sister Grace Marie Schutte speaks of the "two moments" in prayer: reflection and engagement.[26] In her view, vocal prayer is primarily dialogue with the world and neighbor when engaged in service. R. Gregor Smith redefines prayer as the movement of the whole life in the direction of the reality of God. Gert Otto, German radical theologian, sees prayer as identical with the quest for a responsible form of life.[27] For the liberation theologian Jürgen Moltmann, whose theology bears the imprint of Hegelian philosophy, God is "an event" within history, not "a person projected in heaven."[28] It is therefore not permissible to pray *to* God; instead, we should pray *in* God, in the event of creative love.

The notes of biblical realism and personalism are more readily discernible in David Willis' *Daring Prayer*.[29] Yet his claim that prayer does not change things but changes people who change things tends to naturalize prayer by making it confirm what is explicable in human terms. The idea of a God who decisively intervenes in the affairs of humankind in direct answer to prayer fades into the background in his theology of prayer.

As we examine spiritualistic movements today, we again detect certain emphases that are not in harmony with biblical faith. In Moral Re-Armament, prayer is waiting for guidance. This is considered "scientific prayer," because it can be verified by practical results. In prayer, we do not talk with God but wait for God to talk with us. The charismatic movement tends to denigrate petitionary and rational prayer. Kenneth Hagin advocates that the Christian "exchange petition for praise."[30] According to Merlin Carothers, praise should be given to God for all things, good and bad. It is theologically more appropriate to contend that one should praise God in all circumstances of life, but surely not for evil. We thank God for his presence in evil but not for the evil that falls upon us (cf. Eph. 5:15–20; Ps. 34:1, LB).

This is not to underestimate the evangelical and biblical thrust of the charismatic or Neo-Pentecostal movement. Many people, both Catholic and Protestant, have been led to a rediscovery of biblical, prophetic prayer through this movement. It can be considered a salutary antidote to the creeping formalism and ritualism that afflict mainline Christianity. At the same time, the discerning Christian will be alert to deviations from the biblical standard in this as in all renewal movements. Where the Holy Spirit is at work, evil spirits will also be at work, and those leaders in the charismatic renewal who are biblically and theologically grounded are very much aware of this fact.

## TOWARD THE RECOVERY OF BIBLICAL PRAYER

While the dominant trend in modern theology is to reduce prayer to a mystical sense of the presence of God, some voices have sounded the call to a rediscovery of the biblical meaning of prayer. Among these is Jacques Ellul, who indicts the current understanding of prayer as a technique or method for gaining security and fulfillment. He reminds us that prayer in the biblical sense finally comes to be "a renunciation of human means. It is not merely the point beyond which I could not go, the limit of my power which dissolves into impotence, but it is indeed a stripping bare, the abandonment of all human apparatus in order to place myself, without arms or equipment, into the hands of the Lord, who decides and fulfills."[31]

Karl Barth understands prayer as both gift and obedience. "Prayer," he says, "is the extreme case of God's grace for us," but it is also the invitation to life with and for God. For Barth, there can be no theology apart from commitment and prayer: "The first and basic act of theological work is *prayer*."[32]

Against those who seek to transcend the prayer of petition in mystical rapture and contemplation, H. H. Farmer contends that while petition is not the only element it is "the heart and centre of prayer."[33] When petition is left out, we come to regard prayer as spiritual self-help or adjustment to a semipersonal or impersonal God. He points out that the "suggestion that petitionary prayer is superfluous inasmuch as God's holy purpose is already directed to our good and is seeking in all things to flow into and take possession of our being, entirely overlooks the possibility that the divine purpose may be such that petitionary prayer is indispensable to its realisation."[34]

It is not only orthodox and neo-orthodox theologians who are skeptical of the modern reconception of prayer. Opposing those who see prayer as a technique for self-improvement, Deane William Ferm, who stands in the tradition of theological liberalism, vigorously asserts, "The essence of prayer is not primarily autosuggestion or consciousness-raising but rather communication with God."[35]

Christian prayer is born out of the realization that human beings in and of themselves are incapable of saving themselves from the forces of darkness within and about them. In genuine prayer, we come to God with empty hands trusting solely in his mercy. "The man who really prays," says Karl Barth, "never attempts to justify himself. In true prayer, he knows that he cannot do so."[36] Yet in another sense we also come before the throne of God with full hands, full of the promises of God. We come empty of things but full of faith and hope. We do not bring God offerings that can win his favor, but we do bring before him the petition of an earnest heart.

Prayer understood as the pouring out of the soul before God is indissolubly related to faith. Calvin called prayer "the soul of faith." For Richard Sibbes, "prayer is . . . the voice of faith, the flame of faith."[37] "If we have faith," he said, "we will pray; the more faith the more prayer; the greater faith the greater prayer."[38] Prayer exercises faith just as faith informs prayer. Auguste Sabatier wisely observed that "where there is no prayer from the heart there is no religion."[39]

What Friedrich Heiler calls "ritual prayer" has more to do with the mind than the heart. Saying prayers may be a salutary practice, but it is not yet true prayer. Prayer will inevitably assume a structured pattern, and this is particularly the case in public worship. Yet we must never mistake the visible forms of expression for the spiritual encounter that is invisible to the naked eye.

Similarly, Christian prayer must always be distinguished from primitive prayer. It is necessary to be cognizant of this distinction, for prophetic and primitive prayer have much in common, including a realistic sense of the presence of a living God. Yet, whereas primitive prayer is based exclusively on fear and need, Christian prayer arises out of love and faith as well. The element of need is always present, but it is a need illumined by faith and subordinated to the will and glory of God. In primitive prayer, we confess mistakes but not sin; in Christian prayer on the other hand, we are keenly aware of our moral turpitude in the sight of God and ask for his cleansing and mercy. In primitive religion, prayer is a technique based on the supposition that human beings can have power over God. Primitive people seek to gain possession of divine power and use it for their own purposes. Prayer is seen as a natural achievement that one can take pride in if the desired results are readily discernible. In Christianity, on the contrary, prayer is the miracle of God's intervening grace. We can pray fervently for this intervention, but we cannot force the hand of God.

## REAPPRAISING MENTAL PRAYER

Mental prayer or meditation is not a substitute for true prayer, nor is it to be regarded as a higher form of prayer. Yet rightly understood it can be a powerful aid in prayer. It can be a preparation for prayer as well as a supplement to it.

Thomas Merton, in his *Contemplative Prayer*, reminds us that the church fathers and early monks constantly meditated on Scripture.[40] To be sure, many of them saw this meditation as only a means to transcend words altogether and lose themselves in ecstatic union with God. At the same time, it cannot be denied that a deep love for the Bible was fostered in the monastic orders and that meditation on Scripture facilitated the spontaneous supplications that most of them uttered in private.

The great saints of Protestantism, including the Reformers, made a real place for meditation as well as vocal prayer. Henry Scougal confessed, "This mental prayer is of all others the most effectual to purify the soul, and dispose it unto a holy and religious temper, and may be termed the great secret of devotion and one of the most powerful instruments of the divine life."[41]

Evangelical meditation is centered on the works and acts of God not only in creation but also and preeminently in Jesus Christ. Such meditation is intended to bear fruit in loving action and service. In meditation we are convicted of our sins and then spurred to action.

The religious community movement within evangelical Protestantism today is sounding the call to a recovery of meditation as well as a rediscovery of the meaning of biblical prayer. Mother Basilea Schlink of the Evangelical Sisterhood of Mary has declared, "The measure of your service will be according to the measure of your devotion to the hidden service of prayer. According to your prayer will your fruits be."[42] By prayer she has in mind not only talking to God audibly but the communion of the heart with God in silence.

Speaking out of the tradition of prophetic prayer, Ellul claims that "prayer is not the form of man's transfiguration. It is the testimony of the nearness of God who comes."[43] Yet we must ask whether prayer does not indeed effect our transfiguration. Wherever God is present, we are changed, and not just in our attitudes and vision but in our innermost being. Are not the mystics partially right in maintaining that God descends to us so that we may rise to be like God? Evangelical theology is averse to speaking of the deification of humanity, as did the church fathers, since this tends to deny the discontinuity between God the Creator and man the creature. But it is insistent that through prayer we are sanctified, that we are on the way to becoming free for service and obedience. Prayer is the key to the breakthrough into freedom, to the victorious life, which is not yet the perfected life but which is on the way to perfection.

The mystic goal of contemplative adoration as the loss of self in the glory of God is to be contrasted with the prophetic goal of the manifestation of the power of God in human life. This or a similar distinction is frequently made especially by Protestant theologians in the Reformation tradition. Yet we must ask whether there can be a place for the contemplative adoration of God in the biblical sense. Surely some of the Psalms include such an emphasis, though our reflection is directed not to the infinite being of God beyond the world (as in certain kinds of mysticism) but to the glory of God manifested in his works of creation and redemption (cf. Pss. 8, 9, 24, 30, 47, 103, 135, 138, 148). More will be said on the subject of meditation and contemplation in Chapter 6.

Anti-mystical theologians such as Ritschl and Nygren emphasize the service of God in the world to the detriment of the inner life with God in the depths of the soul. Nygren, in his *Agape and Eros*, has made an important distinction between the two types of love, the New Testament Agape, which goes out to the undeserving, and the Greek Eros, which seeks the realization and transformation of the self in union with God.[44] Yet Nygren allows no real place for love toward God, only love toward the neighbor. This patently contradicts the New Testament theme that love for God takes priority even over love for neighbor. Love for God in the Christian sense is not self-serving natural love but self-giving spiritual love that includes compassion for others. Indeed, we seek to serve our neighbor for the glory of God, so that God's Word might be exalted and honored. And

God seeks his own glory for the sake of the world, for its redemption and sanctification. True love is not a flight from the world into ecstatic union with the divine but the upholding and serving of the divine revelation in the midst of the world's anguish. True love is not simply sharing the fruits of our contemplation with those less fortunate (as certain mystics sometimes express it) but also constantly identifying with the unfortunate in their tribulation and thereby giving visible manifestation to our love for Christ before the world.

## NOTES

1. "Can Modern Man Pray?" *Newsweek,* 72, no. 27 (1968): 38.
2. Charles Fager, "Drinan Sees Mandate 'to Resist Nixon,' " *National Catholic Reporter,* 9, no. 13 (1973): 6.
3. Thomas Molnar documents a movement away from the Left among France's intellectual and cultural elite, but many of those who have gravitated toward the ideological Right remain anti-Christian as well as anti-American. See Thomas Molnar, "A Cultural Coup d'Etat," *National Review,* 30, no. 47 (1978): 1481–1482.
4. Ralph C. Wood, " 'Innocents Abroad' No More," *The Christian Century,* 95, no. 23 (1978): 677.
5. Harry Blamires, *The Faith and Modern Error* (London: S.P.C.K., 1964), p. 128.
6. Ronald Gregor Smith, *Secular Christianity* (New York: Harper & Row, 1966), p. 207.
7. Jacques Ellul, *Prayer and Modern Man,* trans. C. Edward Hopkin (New York: Seabury Press, 1970), p. 100.
8. Helmut Thielicke, *The Evangelical Faith,* trans. G. W. Bromiley (Grand Rapids, Mich.: Eerdmans, 1974), Vol. 1, p. 114.
9. See E. Harold Smith, "The Catholic Crisis," *Commonweal,* 95, no. 14 (1972): 322.
10. Henry Wood, *The New Thought Simplified* (Boston: Lee & Shepard, 1903), p. 107.
11. Merlin Carothers, *Praise Works!* (Plainfield, N.J.: Logos International, 1973).
12. That strand in the charismatic movement that is more biblically informed (as, for example, in Thomas Smail and J. Rodman Williams) acknowledges the temptation to magic in the life of prayer and warns against it.
13. Mary Baker Eddy, *Science and Health with Key to the Scriptures* (Boston: Trustees under the will of Mary Baker G. Eddy, 1934), p. 7.

14. Annie Besant, *The Changing World* (Chicago: Theosophical Press, 1909), p. 68.
15. John Macquarrie, *Paths in Spirituality* (New York: Harper & Row, 1972), p. 27.
16. Gregory Baum, *Man Becoming: God in Secular Experience* (New York: Herder & Herder, 1970), p. 264.
17. Matthew Fox, *On Becoming a Musical, Mystical Bear* (New York: Harper & Row, 1972), pp. 16 ff., 49 ff. According to Fox, prayer is a response not to God, but to the mysteries of life. Fox draws upon mysticism, existentialism, and process thought.
18. Michael Novak, *All the Catholic People* (New York: Herder & Herder, 1971), p. 106.
19. Don Brophy, "Why I Don't Pray Anymore," *National Catholic Reporter*, 10, no. 18 (1974): 12.
20. Cited in *The Presbyterian Journal*, 27, no. 41 (1969): 12.
21. Paul Tillich, *Systematic Theology* (Chicago: University of Chicago Press, 1963), Vol. 3, pp. 116–120, 190–193, 279–280.
22. Karl Jaspers, *The Perennial Scope of Philosophy*, trans. Ralph Manheim (New York: Philosophical Library, 1949), p. 82.
23. J. A. T. Robinson, *Exploration into God* (Stanford, Calif.: Stanford University Press, 1967), p. 123.
24. J. A. T. Robinson, *Honest to God* (Philadelphia: Westminster Press, 1963), p. 105.
25. Douglas Rhymes, *Prayer in the Secular City* (Philadelphia: Westminster Press, 1967), p. 70.
26. Sister Grace Marie Schutte, "Reflections on Prayer and Worldly Holiness," *Worship*, 41, no. 2, (1967): 108–112.
27. See Heinrich Ott, *God* (Richmond: John Knox Press, 1974), pp. 90 ff.
28. Jürgen Moltmann, *The Crucified God*, trans. R. A. Wilson and John Bowden (New York: Harper & Row, 1974), p. 247.
29. David Willis, *Daring Prayer* (Atlanta, Ga.: John Knox Press, 1977). Willis' basic biblical orientation is slightly compromised by his aligning himself with Tillich's attempt to deliteralize the biblical "myth."
30. Kenneth E. Hagin, *Praying to Get Results* (Tulsa, Okla.: Kenneth Hagin Evangelistic Association, 1974), pp. 9 ff.
31. Ellul, *Prayer and Modern Man*, p. 30.
32. Karl Barth, *Evangelical Theology*, trans. Grover Foley (Garden City, N.Y.: Doubleday, Anchor Books, 1964), p. 160.
33. Herbert H. Farmer, *The World and God* (London: Nisbet, 1936), p. 134.
34. *Ibid.*, p. 138.
35. Deane William Ferm, "The Abuse of God," *The Christian Century*, 92, no. 11 (1975): 308.
36. Karl Barth, *Church Dogmatics*, ed. G. W. Bromiley and T. F. Torrance, Vol. II, 2 (Edinburgh: Clark, 1957), p. 752.
37. Richard Sibbes, *The Complete Works of Richard Sibbes*, ed. Alexander Balloch Grosart (Edinburgh: Nichol, 1862–64), Vol. 3, p. 185. Cf. "Prayer and

faith are all one, prayer being nothing but faith digested into words and conceptions" *(Complete Works,* Vol. 4, p. 453).
38. Sibbes, *Complete Works,* Vol. 3, p. 191.
39. Cited in Olive Wyon, *The School of Prayer* (New York: Macmillan, 1966), p. 5.
40. Thomas Merton, *Contemplative Prayer* (Garden City, N.Y.: Doubleday Image Books, 1971).
41. Henry Scougal, *The Life of God in the Soul of Man* (London: InterVarsity Fellowship, 1962), p. 78.
42. Mother Basilea Schlink, *Rules for the Servants of God* (Darmstadt-Eberstadt: Oekumenische Marienschwesternschaft, 1956). (Pamphlet.)
43. Ellul, *Prayer and Modern Man,* p. 48.
44. Anders Nygren, *Agape and Eros,* trans. Philip S. Watson (Philadelphia: Westminster Press, 1953).

# The Scriptural Basis of Prayer

## THE LIVING AND ALMIGHTY GOD

Christian prayer rests upon the irreversible fact of the self-revelation of God in Jesus Christ and its confirmation in our hearts by the Holy Spirit. The Holy Trinity is the basis of true prayer as well as its goal. Prayer, as biblical faith understands it, is made possible by the triune God and is directed to this God.

To gain a true awareness of the depth and breadth of Christian prayer, it is necessary to understand something of the nature of the God who originates such prayer. This God is first of all a Personal Spirit who is self-sustaining and who is the ground of everything that is. He not only exists but he also coexists as a Trinity. He is capable of having fellowship with humanity because he has fellowship within himself. He is capable of caring because he embodies love within himself.

The God of the Bible is a living God, not a philosophical first principle or a moral ideal. As the psalmist expresses it, "He who planted the ear, does he not hear? He who formed the eye, does he not see?" (Ps. 94:9). He is not divinity in the abstract, but a divine person. He is supremely personal, yet he infinitely transcends human personhood. He is a personal-infinite God (Francis Schaeffer), who is at the same time all-powerful and all-loving. He is a gregarious God, seeking to include man in fellowship with himself. Such a God can be approached in prayer because he not only can hear but also has the power to act on the requests of his children.

The biblical picture of God as "heavenly Father" reinforces the idea that he is loving and caring. We do not ask as beggars but as sons and daughters, since he is the Father of all by creation and the Father of Christians in particular by adoption. God is also likened in the Bible to a divine Mother who seeks to gather her children together as a hen would gather her brood under her wings (Matt. 23:37).

In the Christian tradition, some mystics have sought to transcend the Trinity by positing a "God above God," an infinite abyss that lies beyond personality and diversity. The God that is thus depicted is incontestably other than the God of Abraham, Isaac, and Jacob: he resembles more the Prime Mover or Infinite One of Hellenistic philosophy. Such a God transcends pity as well as anger. He is infinitely removed from temporality as well as materiality. This is the God described by the seventeenth-century mystical poet, Angelus Silesius: "How often have I prayed 'Lord do your will'. . . . But see: He does no willing—motionless He is and still."[1] Far from being a static absolute beyond history, the God of the Bible is living and dynamic will who enters into history in order to have fellowship with his people.

Nor is God a creative process that perpetually resides in nature and that includes the totality of nature within his own being. In this process view, God moves the world by the magnetic lure that he exercises upon the entities of nature (a conception not very different from Aristotle's). In the biblical view, on the contrary, God is the Almighty One who constantly intervenes in history and who operates in the world as an active power. The totally inclusive God of process philosophy is as far removed from Judeo-Christian faith as the totally impassible God of classical thought.[2]

Against all kinds of idealism and monistic mysticism, Romano Guardini declares:

The words of the "Our Father" tell us: You have to deal not merely with "the Divine"; not merely with a mysterious, all-pervading Deity, but with a Being; not merely with a Something which you can feel, but with a Someone Whom you can address; not merely with an Authority Which touches you but with a Countenance Which you are called to look upon.[3]

The God of the Bible is depicted not only as the Personal Spirit with whom we can have fellowship: he is also the One whose presence is ever recurring and inescapable. He is aptly described in theology as omnipresent. He is not only *about* us and *above* us but also *within* us (Eph. 4:6). He is not only the Supreme Being but at the same time the ground and center of every being. He is closer to us than we are to ourselves (Augustine). He is not a part of us, but he is with us and for us. He is in us, not as an aspect of our being, but as the living center of our existence. He is not spatially in everything (for this would be pantheism), but everything is accessible to his Spirit. Even though he is ever present, it is proper to invoke him because it is common courtesy to invite someone into a conversation, even though that person may be nearby.

Again, the true God is omniscient. He sees all and knows all: "The eyes of the Lord are everywhere, surveying evil and good men alike" (Prov. 15:3 NEB; cf. 2 Chron. 16:9). He knows our needs before we bring them to him (Matt. 6:8). "Even before a word is on my tongue," confesses the psalmist, "lo, O Lord, thou knowest it altogether" (Ps. 139:4). His understanding is "beyond measure" (Ps. 147:5). Yet it pleases him when we acknowledge him as our Father and request his aid and guidance. "Love loves to be told what it knows already"; it "wants to be asked for what it longs to give."[4]

The living and almighty God of the Scriptures knows the course of the future and the fulfillment of the future (including all details), but he does not know *literally* every single event until it happens. He knows every alternative and also exactly what will eventuate, but he does not know this experientially or concretely until he acts in and through the particular event in question.

God is disposed to bring about what he foreordains in conjunction with the actions of men and women, who in themselves are free agents. His grace does not overthrow human freedom but fulfills and directs it. Indeed, God sends his grace upon us to convert our freedom toward a higher purpose and goal. His plan is predetermined, but the way in which he realizes this plan depends partly on the free cooperation of his children. This is not to deny that on occasion God chooses to accomplish his purposes in opposition to the efforts and strivings of his people, but he nevertheless takes these into account in his work of preservation and redemption. Paradoxically we enter into true freedom only by doing the will of God, only by living in obedience to his commands; we fall away from our freedom when we reject and defy the grace of God.

To affirm an omniscient God has far-reaching practical implications for the life of prayer. It means that absolute honesty is called for, since God knows our innermost thoughts and needs. Indeed, sometimes our prayers are answered even before they are uttered (cf. Isa. 65:24). Augustine declares with keen perception, "God does not ask us to tell him our needs that he may learn about them, but in order that we may be capable of receiving what he is preparing to give."[5]

As has already been indicated, the God of biblical revelation is all-powerful (omnipotent). He is sovereign over history as well as immanent within history. He can and does answer every request made in the name of Jesus Christ. Yet he chooses to answer in his own way and in his own time. He answers according to his holy will and not necessarily according to what we desire or demand. He is not inherently dependent on us, but he makes himself dependent in order to work out his purposes in the role of a covenant partner. His sovereignty is not compromised but confirmed in his condescension to a sinful humanity.

When I contend that God is all-powerful, I do not mean that he is a God of arbitrary power. More properly he is the God of conquering love. His power does not violate his love; instead it is in the service of his love. The God of the Bible does not contradict his own nature: he remains true to himself. Because he is faithful to himself, to his Word, to his promises, we can enter confidently into prayer with him, knowing that he will remain faithful in answering our requests, in fulfilling our legitimate needs and desires.

The God of revelation is also transcendent. He is the Creator, we are only finite creatures. Although he comes into us by his Spirit, he is never a part of us. Although he is the center of our being, he is not accessible to us except as he makes himself accessible. He is hidden from all sight and understanding (Isa. 50:10; 1 Cor. 2:9–11). Because he is enveloped in mystery, he must be approached in awe and reverence. He is a supernatural God, one who exists beyond all finite existence. One reason for the incarnation is that he had to become like us so that we could know him and enter into fellowship with him.

The true God is neither distant (as in deism) nor directly accessible (as in pantheism or panentheism). He is imminent, very near but also eminent—much more lofty than man. Yet this in no way limits his contact with us. He is present *to* the world, not confined within the world.

Besides being the "Wholly Other," God is also the Holy One who has an abiding hatred of sin; he must therefore be approached in penitence, even in fear and trembling. The living God of the Bible is a consuming fire who purges and judges us in our sins. This is why as sinful human beings we stand in need of a mediator, one who will intercede for us and expiate our guilt. As Christians we believe that we can stand before the throne of God only on the basis of the alien righteousness of Jesus Christ, which alone satisfies the just requirements of God's law and thereby atones for sin.

Not that God was obliged to provide a mediator for sinful humankind. Rather in his sovereign freedom he chose to do so, moved only by his boundless compassion. The freedom of God implies that he is not under any external constraint or metaphysical necessity.

It must also be asserted that this God who acts in freedom is above human law and logic. In Isaiah we read, "My thoughts are not your thoughts, neither are your ways my ways, says the Lord. For as the heavens are higher than the earth, so are my ways higher than your ways and my thoughts than your thoughts" (55:8,9). This does not mean that God's ways remain totally hidden from human understanding, for God has revealed himself not only in Christ but in the testimony of the Scriptures. Yet it does mean that our understanding and conceptualization of God's self-revelation can never be exhaustive, nor can our language about God ever be univocal. We see only as through a glass darkly; we know by the analogy of faith, not by the literal predication of reason.

As the God of sovereign freedom, he is not bound to any means or instruments which he might happen to use. His actions do not fit into any physical or "spiritual" laws that we can discover or conceive. He cannot be manipulated or managed. He has made his Word the instrument for our salvation, and he is bound to the Word in this respect, but he is not confined to it. He goes beyond what he has promised, and he realizes his purposes in ever new ways. He is always faithful to himself and to his word. But if we do not live up to our responsibility in the covenant, then he is free to implement his promises in a way that will bring sorrow rather than joy upon us. As the God who is free to withdraw himself as well as give of himself, he cannot be taken for granted. Although he is always merciful, we must plead for his mercy ever again if we are to experience it fully.

Finally, we come to the affirmation that God is love. Even as he is essentially holiness, so also he is essentially love. As the God of love he is merciful, compassionate, solicitous. He will listen to us even while we are yet in our sins. He has accepted us in the person of Jesus Christ, even though we are basically unworthy. He accepts us now through his Spirit even when we may not be able to accept ourselves. We need have no compunction in revealing to him our inmost needs and desires and in sharing with him our deepest thoughts, even when these are intolerable and unthinkable. In sharing them with God we are released from their power. Luther once said that prayer gives to the Christian the "power to bear his troubles and to overcome them."

While we proclaim that God is love, we must not mistake love for God. God is love, but he is more than love: he is holy will and dynamic energy. He is a divine person who loves, but he is also free to act in a way contrary to the human understanding of love. He is a God of holy love, a love whose severity sharply distinguishes it from the purely sentimental love of popular fiction. As the God of holy love, he transcends the moral understood as a rational ideal. His being contains that aspect of the holy which Rudolf Otto calls "the numinous," the nonrational that transcends goodness as a general principle.[6]

All the perfections of God are revealed and exemplified in Jesus Christ, God incarnate in human flesh. In Christ we see God's wrath against sin, but we also perceive his love that goes out to the most unworthy of sinners. We discern his power revealed in the weakness of the cross, his lordship manifested in the role of servanthood. In the cross we realize that his omnipotence is one of love. As Catherine of Siena put it so forcefully: "Nails were not enough to hold God-and-Man nailed and fastened to the Cross, had Love not held Him there."[7] His freedom was revealed as a freedom to be *with* us and *for* us even unto death. This is indeed the kind of God that can be solicited in prayer, for we know that his power is informed by mercy and that his glory is his overflowing love, the grace that goes out to the undeserving.

One question that is often asked has considerable bearing on the life of prayer: How is it possible to reconcile an all-powerful and loving God with evil? I contend that though nothing happens apart from God's will, not everything that happens is God's will. Evil, sin, and sickness are manifestly what God does not will. Yet they could not happen apart from his permission, even his sanction. He allows evil to have a provisional reality so that his power might be demonstrated against it and so that greater good might eventuate. Evil is not God's will but that we are brought into contact with evil is his will. He uses evil to bring evil to nought. God is not the direct cause of evil, but he is the cause of the overthrow of evil. This means that in our prayer life we should not meekly submit to evil but instead boldly lay hold of the power of God to combat evil and overcome it.

It is important to realize that there is another power at work in the universe, the devil. The Bible makes unmistakably clear that behind the tribulation and discord in the world is a demonic adversary of God and man. He is a divine anti-divine being, superior to man but inferior to God. Yet behind the work of the devil is the wrath of God, for God is still ultimately in control. Indeed, God accomplishes his secret will through the perverse will of the devil. God works through the devil but not in the same way as he works through the church or the Word. Luther rightly distinguished between the alien work of God, by which he brings suffering and tribulation, and his proper work, by which he offers mercy and salvation. Sometimes it seems that God must do the former before he can do the latter. When we (or the devil) do injury to others it is dirty work; when God does it, it is holy work. The reason is, of course, that God does it with a holy motivation, to purge people of sin and to prepare them for redemption.

## THE DECISIVE ROLE OF JESUS CHRIST

Christian prayer has its basis not only in God the Father but also in his Son, Jesus Christ, apart from whose mediation and intercession we would not be able to come before the throne of grace. Because of our sins, we would have no guarantee that our prayers would be heard unless there were a Mediator to speak for us. As it is said, "Thou hast wrapped thyself with a cloud so that no prayer can pass through" (Lam. 3:44). Yet because of the vicarious atonement of Jesus Christ, because of his substitutionary death on the cross and his resurrection from the grave, the guilt and penalty of sin have been removed from the human race. If we believe, we can now approach God assured that our petitions will be heard because they are united with the sacrificial offering of the One whose righteousness covers our sins. Because he is our Representative as well as our Substitute, we now have access to the throne of God.

In anticipation of the revelation of Christ, Daniel acknowledged that "we do not present our supplications before thee on the ground of our righteousness, but on the ground of thy great mercy" (Dan. 9:18). And this mercy was revealed and assured to us in the person of Jesus, in his sacrificial life and death on the cross.

Jesus Christ makes possible the life of genuine prayer first of all in his role as Revealer. He reveals to us the depth and breadth of the mercy of God. He demonstrates for us that God is not only holiness but also boundless compassion. Therefore we should feel free to enter into his presence with our innermost needs and petitions. Because of his power and mercy revealed in Jesus Christ, we can be certain that our prayers will be heard and answered so long as we cling to Christ as our Advocate and Savior.

Secondly, Christ gives reality to the life of prayer in his role as Reconciler. He has overcome the enmity between God and man by making the one sacrifice acceptable to God, a sacrifice on man's behalf. Through his vicarious, substitutionary representation, he has made it possible for God's love to reach sinful humanity, and for our faith to reach a holy God. Whereas once we were alienated from our Creator, we are now restored to fellowship with the divine through the mediation of Jesus Christ who assures us of both justification and sanctification.

Thirdly, Christ establishes the life of prayer in his role as Redeemer. Whereas formerly we were enslaved to powers and forces beyond our control, we have now been liberated from these powers through the cross and resurrection of Jesus Christ from the grave. Christ already triumphed over the powers in his dying on the cross, and he confirmed his triumph through his resurrection from the grave. By bearing the brunt of the attack of the powers of evil in his own person, by not succumbing but remaining in union with God until the end, by demonstrating his power over death and hell in rising from the dead, Christ overthrew the demonic adversary. Paul testifies that God "disarmed the principalities and powers and made a public example of them, triumphing over them in him" (Col. 2:15). The will of sinful humanity has been released from its bondage to the powers of darkness and set free for fellowship with God and for service in his kingdom.

Again, Christ gives our prayers form and substance in his role as Intercessor in heaven. He prays our prayers for us. He unites our prayers with his so that God hears us (cf. Rom. 8:34). Calvin emphasized the crucial work of the intercession of Christ in the life of prayer. According to him, prayer is founded on the intercession of Christ, for "our mouths are not clean enough to sing the praises of God's name until Christ's priesthood intercedes for us."[8] He cited Ambrose with approbation:

> He [Jesus Christ] is our mouth, through which we speak to the Father; he is our eye, through which we see the Father; he is our right hand, through which we offer ourselves to the Father. Unless he intercedes, there is no intercourse with God either for us or for all saints.[9]

For Calvin our prayers can obtain an answer only through God's forgiveness.

Still another way in which Christ makes a genuine prayer life possible is by his dwelling within the hearts of believers. He not only intercedes for us in heaven, but by his Spirit he makes his abode within the deepest recesses of our being. We can therefore call on him with confidence and assurance because he is infinitely near. Paul reminded his hearers, "Do you not realize that Jesus Christ is in you?" (2 Cor. 13:5). Confidently he proclaimed, "Christ in you, the hope of glory" (Col. 1:27). Within the being of every Christian there is an inner light, a voice within, which moves us toward prayer. And this inner presence is an abiding refuge in times of trial and tribulation.

Finally, Christ is our example in prayer. He not only reveals the love and mercy of God, he not only expiates our sin and guilt, he not only intercedes for us in heaven—but he also presents to us a life that is a model in Christian prayer. We read that "in the days of his flesh, Jesus offered up prayers and supplications, with loud cries and tears, to him who was able to save him from death, and he was heard for his godly fear" (Heb. 5:7). He wrestled with God in prayer and did not surrender until he had undergone the agony and joy in the struggle of prayer. It was only after he asked that the cup of suffering be removed from him that he prayed, "Nevertheless not my will, but thine, be done" (Luke 22:42). His prayer contained elements of heartfelt petition as well as thanksgiving, but nowhere do we read that he sought to be taken up into the Eternal or enter into a mystical rapture in the manner of the contemplatives of Eastern religion. Instead of turning his back on the world in a flight to the transcendent, he actively interceded for his people (John 17:6–26). Moreover, he did not call his disciples out of the world, but instead sent them into the midst of the world as heralds, ambassadors, and intercessors (John 17:15–18).

Jesus' prayers were devoid of the egoism and servile weakness that are so often reflected in primitive prayer. His prayer life signified both absolute dependence on God and a confident laying hold of the power of God. Forsyth comments that his prayer "was more full of God's gift of grace than of man's poverty of faith, of a holy love than of a seeking heart."[10] Jesus was tempted to despair, but he never succumbed, always emerging triumphant in his ongoing battle with the powers of darkness. He demonstrated that the life of prayer is a life of victory—over the weakness of the flesh and the wickedness of a fallen world.

Because our Savior plays such a crucial role in the life of prayer, we should always pray having in mind his salvation and intercession. We should pray not only in the spirit of Christ but also in the name of Christ. To pray in the name of Christ means to pray in the awareness that our prayers have no worthiness or efficacy apart from his atoning sacrifice and redemptive mediation. It means to appeal to the blood of Christ as the source of power for the life of prayer. It means to acknowledge our complete helplessness apart from his mediation and intercession. To pray in his name means that we recognize that our prayers cannot penetrate the tribunal of God unless they are presented to the Father by the Son, our one Savior and Redeemer.

## THE OUTPOURING OF THE HOLY SPIRIT

Prayer is grounded not only in God the Father and God the Son but also in God the Holy Spirit. Apart from the outpouring of the Holy Spirit there can be no prayer worthy of the name of Christian. Wherever the Holy Spirit makes his entry into human life, there we find the origin of Christian prayer, since it is the Spirit who moves us to pray and who instructs us in the life of prayer. The outpouring of the Spirit at Pentecost is graphically foretold by Zechariah: "And I will pour upon the house of David, and upon the inhabitants of Jerusalem, the spirit of grace and of supplications" (Zech. 12:10, KJV; cf. Joel 2:28, 29; Isa. 32:14–16; Ezek. 39:28, 29). At the time of Pentecost, the apostles were clothed with power from on high and, overwhelmed by their experience, were moved to give utterance in the language of ecstasy (Acts 2:1–13). Before Pentecost, the disciples prayed out of weakness, but filled with the Holy Spirit they now testified and prayed with power and boldness. Their prayers resembled more a hymn than a cry (cf. Acts 4:23–31). Although they still were moved to confess their needs before God in prayer, their prayer life after Pentecost was kindled by grace more than inspired by fear.

It is the Holy Spirit who unites us with the living Christ and thereby enables us to enter into a living communion with him. It is the Spirit who prays for us and with us (Rom. 8:15, 16). He teaches us how to pray, for we do not know how to pray as we ought (Rom. 8:26). He is the Spirit of wisdom and understand-

ing, the Spirit of counsel and might, the Spirit of knowledge and
the fear of the Lord (Isa. 11:2). It is the Spirit who illumines us
from within, who convicts us of sin and who leads us to the
throne of grace in repentance. Hallesby rightly observes, "The
Spirit of prayer makes us so intimate with God that we scarcely
pass through an experience before we speak to Him about it, either in supplication, in sighing, in pouring out our woes before
Him, in fervent requests, or in thanksgiving and adoration."[11] It
is the Spirit who so impresses upon us the majesty and glory of
God that we are invariably moved to lift up our voices to him in
praise and adoration.[12]

The Spirit plants within us those desires that reside in the inner being of God. As the Puritan father Thomas Goodwin expresses it, the Spirit "who searches the deep things of God, doth
offer, prompt and suggest to us in our prayers those very things
that are in God's heart, to grant the things we desire of Him, so
as it often comes to pass that a poor creature is carried on to
speak God's very heart to Himself, and then God cannot, nor
doth not deny."[13]

True prayer is not taking place unless it is enlivened and directed by the Holy Spirit. Prayer is something more than a discourse or an address directed to God: it is the passionate crying
out of our whole being for God. It is not the mere saying of pray-
erful words but actually speaking with God in the power of the
Spirit. According to Ellul, "Only when the Holy Spirit intercedes, and in a way which *cannot be expressed,* that is, which
transcends all verbalizing, all language, then is the prayer prayer, and it is a relationship with God."[14] Prayer is appropriately
described by Richard Sibbes as "incense kindled by the fire of
the blessed Spirit of God."[15]

In the experience of the baptism of the Spirit, by which we
are united with Christ in his death and resurrection, we are invariably moved to bear witness to our Savior in the language of
prayer. One writer vividly records the impact of the descent of
the Spirit upon the person of faith, showing how this results in a
quickened life of prayer:

My heart now overflows
　With prayers and praises.
My heavenly Father knows
　Each sigh that raises
My heart ever nearer His heart
　so tender;
For there's my joy and peace;
In Thee I've found release,
　My soul's Defender.[16]

With the coming of the Spirit and the awakening to faith, we are now enabled to be conquerors, we are now empowered to live lives of victory over temptation and sin (cf. Rom. 8:37). Sibbes puts this very dramatically: "Where this faith is, *it is a triumphing, a conquering grace, a prevailing grace*. It overcomes the world and whatsoever is opposite, for it sets before the soul greater things than the world can. . . . Faith coming into the soul subdues all to itself, and makes all serviceable."[17] According to Forsyth, "The deeper we go down into the valley of decision the higher we must rise (if we are to possess and command our souls) into the mount of prayer, and we must hold up the hands of those whose chief concern is to prevail with God."[18]

The saints are still aware of their helplessness and infirmity apart from God; they must still approach the throne of the Holy on their knees, but they are now emboldened to speak openly to God about their needs and concerns. They now have the confidence that their prayers will be heard and acted on, that no force in the creaturely heavens or on earth can stand against the power of the Holy Spirit who dwells within all believers.

Although the Holy Spirit abides in the hearts of all those who believe, he must not be taken for granted. We can grieve and quench the Spirit; the Spirit can and does withdraw his aid from us if we turn again to the pathway of sin. Karl Barth gives this apt warning: "Unless the Holy Spirit is sighed for, cried for, prayed for, don't assume that He's present in our organization, in our theology, even in our ordinances."[19] We must pray that the Spirit might manifest his gifts in our lives so that our witness might be credible and compelling, so that our prayers might be meaningful and efficacious.

## PUBLIC AND PRIVATE PRAYER

Christian prayer is both private and public, but it is not exclusively either of these. It is deeply personal, but it is not individualistic. It will invariably assume corporate expression, but the personal element is never missing in true prayer.

Even when prayer is private, it is offered in the body of Christ through the One Spirit who dwells in all the members. Moreover, it is focused not on the needs of the petitioner alone but also on the needs of the community. Forsyth declares that "we are saved in a common salvation. The atmosphere of prayer is communion. Common prayer is the inevitable fruit of a gospel like Christ's."[20] In his view, "private prayer should be common in spirit. We are doing in the act what many are doing."[21]

Daniel Jenkins has suggested that common prayer is the primary form and private prayer only one small aspect of the corporate prayer of the church.[22] Yet he is overstating the case, since the Bible never subordinates the personal prayer of the individual to the collective prayer of the people of God. I agree with Heiler that collective prayer may be a supplement but never a substitute for personal prayer. Ellul rightly asks, "How can we pretend that prayer is *primarily* communal, when to the contrary we see Jesus seeking to be alone and to withdraw from the crowd, even from his own disciples, in order to pray?"[23] Even Forsyth, who emphasizes the communal dimension of prayer, nevertheless remarks, "Private prayer, when it is made a serious business, when it is formed prayer, when we pray audibly in our chamber, or when we write our prayers, guided always by the day's record, the passion of piety, and above all the truths of Scripture, is worth more for our true and grave and individual spirituality than gatherings of greater unction may be."[24]

The prophetic tradition in the Old Testament gave attention to the spontaneous prayer of the heart, the pouring out of the soul before God, but the priestly tradition stressed the need for form and ritual in worship. Already in Leviticus the emphasis was placed on offerings and sacrifice, which in themselves are a dramatic form of prayer. In the priestly period during and after the exile, scriptural terminology was prominent and interest in liturgical propriety intensified. With the loss of the temple, gatherings for prayer and Scripture reading prepared for the development of the synagogue. The vision of a new temple in Ezekiel indicates that worship was thought of as corporate, organized under a priesthood.

At the same time, it cannot be denied that the saints of the Old Testament most often found God in solitude. We need only think of Abraham, who kept a lonely vigil over his sacrifice; Moses at the burning bush; Elijah on Mount Carmel and in the mouth of the cave; Hezekiah with his face to the wall praying for his recovery from an insidious illness; David lying all night on the ground interceding for the health of the child that Bathsheba bore him; and Daniel on his knees alone facing Jerusalem.

In the New Testament, both private and common prayer abound. We read that Jesus prayed with his disciples and taught that there is special power when Christians are united in prayer (Matt. 18:19, 20). The early Christians came together for the breaking of bread and prayers (Acts 2:42). Yet there is also a call to solitary prayer. Jesus advised his disciples not to stand and pray in the synagogues and at street corners, where they would be seen by people, but instead to go into their own rooms and shut the door and pray to their Father in secret (Matt. 6:5, 6). Jesus himself often withdrew from the company of his disciples in order to be alone with God, and his deepest encounters with the Holy came in such periods. Paul was confronted by Christ on the road to Damascus, and his companions did not share in this experience; Peter received a vision from God on the house-top at Joppa; and John was enwrapped in meditation and prayer on the lonely isle of Patmos. Surely the prayer of Jesus in the Garden of Gethsemane attests the cruciality of personal, private prayer.

There is no doubt that both private and public prayer are necessary in the life of the Christian. Yet this private prayer is never exclusively individual nor is this public prayer ever merely formal but always deeply personal.

Although prayer at its best is voluntary and spontaneous, liturgical worship in some form will inevitably arise when believers come together to share their faith and unite their voices in praise to God. As Forsyth observes, "The more it really is common prayer, and the more our relations with men extend and deepen . . . the more we need forms which proceed from the common and corporate conscience of the Church."[25] Christ himself frequently drew on the liturgy of his people, the Psalms.

Prayer that is said in a public assembly on behalf of the whole people of God need not be ritual prayer; it can still come from the heart and be uttered in the power of the Spirit. Even read prayer need not necessarily be empty of existential meaning and spiritual depth. At the same time, it cannot be denied that a creeping formalism can be baneful to the life of prayer and worship. Although James Denney here reflects a low-church bias, his warning contains an element of truth: "A liturgy, however beautiful, is a melancholy witness to the quenching of the Spirit: it may be better or worse than the prayers of one man, but it could never compare for fervour with the spontaneous prayers of a living church."[26]

This is not to assume that extemporaneous prayer from the pulpit is necessarily closer to the ideal of prophetic prayer than a prepared or recited liturgical prayer. Prophetic prayer is voluntary and spontaneous, but it is at the same time from the heart; it involves the whole being of the petitioner as he expresses deeply felt yearnings and groanings within him that have their source and ground in the Spirit of God. Extemporaneous prayer that simply repeats time-worn clichés is none other than a throwback to a ritualistic form of primitive prayer. When uttered from the pulpit, such prayer is a form of spiritual exhibitionism, which is totally alien to the biblical tradition of prayer.

Prophetic prayer in the true sense is rare and difficult, for it commands the whole attention of the petitioner, and it arises out of a deep-felt distress and need as well as a daring faith.[27] It is by no means careless and haphazard; at its best, it shows evidence of reverent reflection on the theme of the prayer, and this is especially true when given in public assembly.

Most people both in their private devotions and in public worship need crutches or aids if they are to engage in the act of prayer, and such things must not be denied them. Even those more mature in the faith constantly fall short of the ideal of prophetic prayer and need to rely on a structured form of devotion. At the same time, Christians should not remain with prescribed forms of devotion but should seek once more to come boldly before the throne of grace giving utterance to their needs before God in the power of the Spirit and with the confident expectation that God will surely hear and act on their requests.

Because Christian prayer is not only rooted in the transcendent but is also intimately related to the world of sin and suffering, it will always have far-reaching social consequences. This social dimension in Christian prayer is the key to the revival of the church and the renewal of society. Forsyth points to its socially regenerative power: "Prayer of the right kind, with heart and soul and strength and mind, unites any society in which it prevails with those last powers of moral and social regeneration that settle history and that reside in the creative grace of the Cross, which is God's true omnipotence in the world."[28] Prayer in the Spirit is socially revolutionary because it prepares the way for the advance of the gospel in society, and the gospel carries with it new social values that contain the seeds for a new society based on the righteousness of the kingdom.

In contrast to primitive prayer and mystical prayer, which are both highly individualistic, the prophetic prayer of biblical religion arises from community and serves the renewal of community. Occasional withdrawal from the crowd in order to be alone with God is readily discernible among the prophets of religions of revelation; yet they do not remain in the solitary state but always return to their people with a message that contains social imperatives as well as exhortations to individual repentance. The concern of the prophets is with the manifestation of the righteousness and power of God in society. And this is why prophetic prayer invariably takes corporate form, though without losing its personal basis.

## UNANSWERED PRAYER

We come now to the perplexing question of unanswered prayer. Does God always hear our prayers, or does he occasionally close his ears to our cries for help? The Bible indicates that sometimes God refuses to hear prayers, but there is always an overriding reason.

We can be assured that God will hear our petitions when we ask in faith and sincerity believing that God can answer and fulfill them. Our prayers will have efficacy when we plead not our own worthiness but only the righteousness of Christ. This is why we need to pray in the *name* of Jesus and not simply conclude our prayers in the spirit of Christ. Such prayer is based on the recognition that only Christ's prayer is efficacious for our salvation.

Scripture also tells us that God sometimes hears and answers prayer even where there is little faith or where genuine faith is absent. It appears that if contrition or a genuine plea for help is present, God may very well act on the request. The woman who touched the fringe of Jesus' garment was granted immediate healing, even though she could not yet have known his Messianic identity (Luke 8:43–48). Of the ten lepers who sought and received healing from Jesus, only one, a Samaritan, was said to have had true faith (Luke 17:11–19). The story of Cain's punishment indicates that God sometimes hears the prayers even of the unconverted (Gen. 4:13–16; cf. Gen. 20:3–7).

At the same time, it is made unmistakably clear in the Scriptures that God does not always answer prayers. God spurned the petitions of the priests of Baal because of their gross idolatry

(1 Kings 18). Moreover, God sometimes refuses to hear the prayers of his own children. When his name is blasphemed and his laws are transgressed, then he will withhold his grace and glory. In Isaiah we read, "Even though you make many prayers, I will not listen; your hands are full of blood" (Isa. 1:15). Jeremiah gives a similar admonition: "Even if they fast, I will not listen to their cry for help" (Jer. 14:12, GNB). In Proverbs 28:9 there is a warning that if we turn a deaf ear to the law, even our prayers will become an abomination to God (cf. Prov. 1:28). And in the words of the psalmist: "If I had cherished iniquity in my heart, the Lord would not have listened" (Ps. 66:18). This same note can be detected in the New Testament: "You ask and do not receive, because you ask wrongly, to spend it on your passions" (James 4:3; cf. 1 John 3:21–22).

Enmity with our brother can also be a reason why our prayers may be rejected by God (cf. Matt. 5:21–26). John Wesley advises: "But that your prayer may have its full weight with God, see that ye be in charity with all men. For, otherwise, it is more likely to bring a curse than a blessing on your own head; nor can you expect to receive any blessing from God while you have not charity towards your neighbour."[29] Richard Sibbes sounds a similar note: "God will rather have no sacrifice than no charity."[30]

Doubt is still another obstacle in the life of prayer. "Let him ask in faith, with no doubting," says James, "for he who doubts is like a wave of the sea that is driven and tossed by the wind. For that person must not suppose that a double-minded man, unstable in all his ways, will receive anything from the Lord" (James 1:6–8).

To be unfailingly effective, prayer must be offered in the assurance of faith, for to doubt the ability or mercy of God is to sin against him. We should doubt ourselves, our own piety, our own worthiness, but we should never doubt the promises of God given in Holy Scripture. Luther advises that in our prayers we should exercise "faith and confidence toward God" in such a way "that we do not doubt that we shall be heard."[31] Karl Barth

concurs that assurance is "not merely . . . a laudable but option-
al property" but "a *conditio sine qua non* of true prayer."[32]

Because God is a holy, living God, he is at the same time a
jealous God who will not tolerate disobedience, particularly
when it takes the form of idolatry. He is also jealous because he
is a solicitous God, One who cares for his children. He is jealous
not only for the purpose of preserving his inviolable holiness
and glory but also in order to safeguard the welfare of his children, who only injure themselves when they go astray.

Christian prayer must forever be distinguished from magic.
The true God cannot be manipulated or controlled. He cannot
be put in a box. He is not at our disposal even in his revelation.
There are no automatic guarantees that God will hear our prayers. Even when our prayers are answered, this is to be attributed
to his free grace. Sinful mankind is always dependent on his
mercy.

Because prayer rests on the promise and command of God, it
has power. Prayer indeed is the most powerful and effective instrument of the Spirit of God. Great preaching is born out of
deep prayer. The evangelist Charles Finney often took with him
to his meetings a devout older man whose sole purpose was to
intercede in prayer while Finney was preaching. Finney recognized that his preaching could be effective only through constant prayer. Luther boldly asserted that "through prayer we
share the almightiness of God. . . . Christians who pray are help-
ers and saviors, yea, masters and gods of the world. They are the
legs which bear the world."[33] For him, the prayer of a godly
Christian is "powerful with God" because that person who in
himself is a sinner is now in God's favor by virtue of the atoning
sacrifice of Christ.[34]

The key to effective prayer is reliance on the grace of God revealed in Jesus Christ and communicated by the Holy Spirit.
When we look to our own powers or to human techniques instead of the Holy Spirit, then God closes his ears to our petitions. Hallesby puts it this way: "Our prayers are rendered inef-

fectual in the same degree as they take a different course than that in which the Spirit would lead us. And they become even more impotent when we come in conflict with the Spirit and grieve Him."[35]

Because God is omniscient he is very much aware of all prayer, even that which arises out of disobedience and rebellion. Yet he will act only on those requests that are pleasing to his holy will, especially those that arise out of faith in his Son, Jesus Christ. He is a God who is generous in his grace and love, who will not withhold his mercy from anyone who acknowledges his own unworthiness and cries out for deliverance. Yet in his sovereign freedom God can and does withhold his grace from those whose prayers make a mockery of his laws. As the omnipotent and omniscient God he hears and knows all prayer, but as the holy One who detests all sin and iniquity he will not give an open ear to prayers that arise out of human arrogance and give glory only to man. The throne of God must therefore be approached in fear and trembling born out of the recognition that God is infinite and holy, whereas we are finite and sinful (Isa. 6:5; 66:2). At the same time, because of God's mercy vouchsafed to us in Jesus Christ, we can also come to God confident that his grace is sufficient to cover our sins and that his love is illimitable, encompassing the whole human creation. There are grounds for hope even for the most despicable sinners, because even they have an advocate with the Father, One who has borne their sins and whose mercy is everlasting.

How can we be certain that God has in fact heeded our prayer for deliverance? If we are earnest in our request, if we cry to God from the depths of our hearts, we can be assured that such prayer must have its origin in God and therefore be acceptable to him. According to Sibbes, "Earnestness in prayer is a sign God hears our prayers, as fire kindled from heaven sheweth God accepts the sacrifice. The ground of prevailing by our prayer, is, that they are put up in a gracious name, and for persons in favour, and dictated by God's own Spirit."[36] The very act of throwing ourselves on the mercy of God brings forth the confidence that God looks with favor on our request, since this act could only arise from the outpouring of the Holy Spirit.

## NOTES

1. *The Book of Angelus Silesius,* trans. Frederick Franck (New York: Vintage Books, 1976), p. 93.
2. For a discerning study on how the God of neoclassicism (process thought) differs from the God of the Bible, see Colin E. Gunton, *Becoming and Being* (Oxford: Oxford University Press, 1978). Gunton points out the similarities between the classical and neoclassical view as opposed to the biblical view. Process thought as well as classical thought seeks a God that transcends the human emotions of pity and anger. The process theology of Hartshorne and Whitehead is both idealistic and naturalistic in that it posits the world of nature as the only reality, but it sees nature as permeated by mind.
3. Romano Guardini, *The Lord's Prayer,* trans. Isabel McHugh (New York: Pantheon Books, 1958), p. 23.
4. P. T. Forsyth, *The Soul of Prayer,* 5th ed. (London: Independent Press, 1966), p. 63.
5. Augustine, *Letters,* 130, p. 17.
6. See Rudolf Otto, *The Idea of the Holy,* trans. John W. Harvey (New York: Oxford University Press, 1958).
7. Cited in Olive Wyon, *The School of Prayer* (New York: Macmillan, 1963), p. 82
8. John Calvin, *Institutes of the Christian Religion,* ed. John McNeill, trans. Ford Lewis Battles (Philadelphia: Westminster Press, 1960), III, 20, 28, p. 890.
9. Calvin, *Institutes III,* 20, 21, p. 879. See also Ambrose, *On Isaac or the Soul,* viii, 75 J.-P. Migne, *Patrologia Latina* 14, p. 557.
10. Forsyth, *The Soul of Prayer,* p. 41.
11. O. Hallesby, *Prayer,* trans. Clarence Carlsen (Minneapolis: Augsburg, 1931), p. 172.
12. Cf. Luther: "Wherever the spirit of grace resides, there we can and dare, yes, must begin to pray." *Luther's Works,* ed. Jaroslav Pelikan Vol. 24 (St. Louis: Concordia, 1961), p. 88.
13. Cited in D. M. McIntyre, *In His Likeness* (London: Marshall, Morgan & Scott, n.d.), p. 28.
14. Jacques Ellul, *Prayer and Modern Man,* trans. C. Edward Hopkin (New York: Seabury Press, 1970), p. 62.
15. Richard Sibbes, *The Complete Works of Richard Sibbes,* ed. Alexander Balloch Grosart (Edinburgh: Nichol, 1862–1864), Vol. 3, p. 192.
16. Cited in Hallesby, *Prayer,* p. 176.

17. Sibbes, *Complete Works,* Vol. 5, p. 522.
18. Forsyth, *The Soul of Prayer,* p. 53.
19. Cited in *Christian Life,* 40, no. 3 (1978): 25.
20. Forsyth, *The Soul of Prayer,* p. 39.
21. *Ibid.,* p. 40.
22. Daniel Jenkins, *Prayer and the Service of God* (London: Faber & Faber, 1944), p. 107.
23. Ellul, *Prayer and Modern Man,* p. 118.
24. Forsyth, *The Soul of Prayer,* p. 46.
25. *Ibid.,* p. 39.
26. Cited in J. Oswald Sanders, *The Holy Spirit and His Gifts* (Grand Rapids, Mich.: Zondervan, 1970), p. 99.
27. Cf. Luther: "It is exceedingly difficult and an art above all arts to pray in the right way, not because of the words or the mouth but for the heart to reach a sure and firm conclusion and to step before God with all confidence." *Luther's Works,* ed. J. Pelikan, Vol. 24, p. 386.
28. Forsyth, *The Soul of Prayer,* p. 56.
29. *John Wesley's Forty-Four Sermons,* 12th impression (London: Epworth Press, 1975), p. 348.
30. Sibbes, *Complete Works,* Vol. 6, p. 167.
31. Hugh Thomson Kerr, Jr., ed., *A Compend of Luther's Theology* (Philadelphia: Westminster Press, 1943), p. 107. Cf. Luther: "A Christian must be as sure of the fulfillment of his prayer as he is of the truthfulness of God." *Luther's Works,* ed. J. Pelikan Vol. 24, p. 394.
32. Karl Barth, *Church Dogmatics,* ed. G. W. Bromiley and T. F. Torrance (Edinburgh: Clark, 1961), Vol. III, 4, p. 107.
33. Cf. "They [Christians] will become gods and will be saviors of the world by their supplication" on behalf of "their neighbor" (*Luther's Works,* Vol. 24, p. 87). He could also say that "the might of prayer" is "so great" that "it has overcome both heaven and earth" (*Luther's Works,* Vol. 6, p. 158). Similarly, Sibbes contends that "what God can do, prayer can do; for prayer binds God, because it is the prayer of faith; and faith, as it were, overcomes God" *Complete Works,* Vol. 6, pp. 106, 107.
34. Kerr, *A Compend of Luther's Theology,* p. 110.
35. Hallesby, *Prayer,* p. 117.
36. Sibbes, *Complete Works,* Vol. 1, p. 256.

# Dialogue with God

## DIALOGIC ENCOUNTER

In the Christian understanding, prayer is the conversation of the heart with God. Gregory of Nyssa called it a conversation and dialogue with God. The Scottish Reformer John Knox defined prayer as "an earnest and familiar talking with God" to whom we make known our miseries, from whom we seek help, and to whom we give praise and thanks.[1] For Calvin, prayer is "a familiar intercourse between God and pious men."[2]

Prayer is something more concrete than communion and union. It is a two-way communication between the Creator and the creature. "To pray," says Heiler, "means to speak to and have intercourse with God."[3] It is not "speech about God" but "speech to God." According to Jacob Boehme, in prayer "a man speaks properly with God and God actually speaks with the soul of man."[4] Ellul sees prayer as a dialogic encounter that is wider and deeper than words. It transcends verbalization but not rationality. The thesis of this book is that true prayer will always give rise to words.

As I see it, there is no such thing as nonthinking prayer in the sense of prayer that is wholly divorced from rational intent. We will always have some intimation of our deepest concerns and needs, even though we may not comprehend them. At the same time, there can be inaudible prayer. In 1 Samuel 1:13, we read,

"Hannah was speaking in her heart; only her lips moved, and her voice was not heard." Although she did not pray aloud, she still prayed with words.

Paul contends that praying in the Spirit should also be praying with the understanding (1 Cor. 14:15). Ideally, the two belong together. Yet he acknowledges the possibility that there can be prayer apart from the understanding, though for him this is not yet complete prayer.

Glossolalia or speaking in tongues is a preparation for prayer, an aid in prayer. Although often described as ecstatic utterance, it is to be understood not as euphoria or intoxication (though this may be involved) but as a state of being lifted above (or outside) rational consciousness. Speaking in tongues may be regarded as a prayer gift that enables the unconscious to express needs and yearnings too deep-seated to be articulated rationally. It is a form of preparatory prayer and therefore incomplete prayer. It becomes complete prayer when the petitioner is given discernment or the gift of interpretation (1 Cor. 14:13 ff.). Then, even though he may be praying in an unknown language, he has a dim perception of the intent of his prayer.[5]

Besides prayer in an unknown ecstatic language, can there be prayer without words? I am thinking here not of mystical prayer but of the Spirit praying in us with sighs too deep for words (Rom. 8:23, 26, 27). Paul implies that we are also active in this form of prayer. We sigh and groan as we are moved by the Spirit. "Nor is prayer ever heard more abundantly," said Luther, "than in such agony and groanings of a struggling faith."[6]

This kind of prayer without words is not beyond intelligibility. It is not the mystical prayer that transcends all conceptualization, but it is the Spirit's urging us in preparation for words. Heiler insists that this wordless groaning is quite different from the *oratio mentalis* of the mystic: "The mystic keeps silence because fixed concentration, meditation and contemplation, are disturbed by speech; the prophet is silent because the emotion is so great that language fails him."[7]

Even though we ourselves may not always grasp the intent

and goal of our sighings and groanings, we may be assured that
they are heard by God so long as we cast ourselves on his mercy
(cf. Ps. 38:8, 9, 15). As Barth phrases it, "It may well be that he
can only sigh, stammer and mutter. But so long as it is a request
brought before God, God will hear it and understand it."[8]

Wordless prayer is present not only when we groan in the
Spirit or give utterance to our need through cries and sobs: it is
also evident when we shout and sing in praise and jubilation.
Ensley maintains that much glossolalia belongs to this tradition
of jubilation, though jubilation as the fathers of the faith generally understood it is wordless vocal prayer, not prayer in an unknown language.[9] The prayer of jubilation is a type of ejacula-
tory prayer, for it consists in spontaneous outbursts of praise
and supplication. Yet it is never divorced from conversation and
address. We shout for joy and then lift up our voices to God in
prayers of praise, adoration and thanksgiving. We may begin to
hum a melody when we do not yet grasp the words to fit the
melody, but the Spirit urges us to express our song in meaningful language so that a real dialogue can take place between God
and ourselves. The spirit of jubilation is reflected in the Living
Bible version of Psalm 28:7: "Joy rises in my heart until I burst
out in songs of praise to him."

Meditation on a spiritual theme is not yet dialogue with God,
and therefore while it may be a salutary exercise in devotion, it
cannot be considered true prayer. Prayer is neither soliloquy
nor self-therapy. It is speaking not to ourselves but to the Wholly Other who encounters the self in its nakedness and misery
and who calls forth a response.

Christian prayer or the prayer of faith is radically different
from the other types of prayer discussed by Heiler, despite some
points of convergence. Christian prayer has a certain affinity to
primitive prayer in that it is spontaneous and voluntary, but its
motivation is not desperation or servile fear but trust and love.
Fear is transformed into awe and reverence because of the deep-
felt sense of the holiness of God, whereas in primitive religion
God is often portrayed as arbitrary and vindictive. Nor can

Christian prayer be equated with ritual prayer in which the repetition of prayer formulas takes the place of a realistic conversation with God. Even less does it resemble philosophic prayer where reflection on the meaning of life or on the worth or identity of the self usurps supplication and petition to a personal God.

Finally, the prayer of faith is to be distinguished from mystical prayer, since it takes the form of dialogue with God and does not seek to transcend the dialogic encounter in ecstatic union with God. In the prayer of faith we are brought into companionship with God, not fusion with him. Such prayer comes from the heart; it involves our whole being. As the psalmist expresses it, "I will give thanks to the Lord with my whole heart" (Ps. 9:1).

Christian prayer is personal, loving address. One does not seek to use God for one's own ends but instead to find out the will of God for one's life. One does not passively resign oneself to the will of God but actively seeks to discover this will and then to apply it to the whole of life.

True dialogue involves complaint and question. According to Ellul, "A dialogue implies reserve, tension, contradiction, argument back and forth."[10] This is conspicuously apparent in Jeremiah 12:1 (GNB): "Lord, if I argued my case with you, you would prove to be right. Yet I must question you about matters of justice. Why are wicked men so prosperous? Why do dishonest men succeed?"

God wants us as covenant partners, not as robots who obey without thinking. He desires that we mean what we pray and therefore disdains vain repetition in prayer (cf. Matt. 6:5–7; cf. Ecclesiasticus 7:14). Jesus likens meaningless repetition to the prayer of the Gentiles (Matt. 6:7). True prayer involves the mind as well as the heart. I cannot agree with Timothy Leary that "to pray properly you must be out of your mind."[11] Some Moslem mystics have also spoken in this fashion. Drugs that induce ecstasy and hallucinations have no place in Christian prayer. Paul acknowledges the rational as well as the voluntaristic element in prayer: "Persevere in prayer, with mind awake and thankful heart" (Col. 4:2, NEB).

Prayer begins in the action of God. The mercy seat in Exodus 25:22 was first to be a place of divine revelation and then a place of intercession for the people of God. At Gibeon the Lord appeared to Solomon in a dream and said, "Ask what I shall give you" (1 Kings 3:5). Only then was Solomon able to enter into meaningful conversation with his God. While still sleeping in the sanctuary, Samuel was summoned by the Lord several times before he responded with the words: "Speak, for thy servant hears" (1 Sam. 3:10). The initiative of God in prayer is graphically depicted in Revelation 3:20: "Behold, I stand at the door and knock; if any one hears my voice and opens the door, I will come in to him and eat with him and he with me."

It is not enough for God to speak to us: he must grant us the power to hear and understand. When God commanded Ezekiel to stand up and listen, the prophet confessed that God's "Spirit entered into me and set me upon my feet; and I heard him speaking to me" (Ezek. 2:1, 2). According to Boehme, the possibility of prayer rests on a divine hearing implanted within us by the grace of God: "Divine hearing is the power of grace . . . by which we are able actually to hear God speaking in us."[12]

From our side, prayer begins in listening and seeking to hear the Word of God. It consists in a response to the voice of God speaking within the depths of our soul. Before there can be meaningful conversation with God, we must take time to wait on the Lord in silent expectation. "Be still before the Lord," says the psalmist, "and wait patiently for him" (Ps. 37:7). And again: "For God alone my soul waits in silence" (Ps. 62:1). Bonhoeffer has rightly observed, "The Word comes not to the chatterer but to him who holds his tongue."[13]

The kind of silence I am advocating should not be confused with the mystical desire to get beyond the Word. It is a waiting on the Word, preparing ourselves to hear the Word. Amy Carmichael offers these words of wisdom:

> Do not be afraid of silence in your prayer time. It may be that you are meant to listen, not to speak. So wait before the Lord. Wait in

stillness. Wait as David waited when he "sat before the Lord." And in that stillness, assurance will come to you. You will know that you are heard; you will know that your Lord ponders the voice of your humble desires; you will hear quiet words spoken to you yourself, perhaps to your grateful surprise and refreshment.[14]

Prayer has two poles, a divine and a human, but the first is prior to the second. Barth perceives that "however difficult it may sound, the hearing really precedes the asking. It is the basis of it. It makes it real asking, the asking of Christian prayer."[15] Similarly, Alfred de Quervain observes, "Prayer is not a means of cultivating God; it is the answer of faith to God's love, truth and goodness, the acknowledgement of God's fatherhood."[16] When God speaks, man is given the capacity and willingness to hear, and when man responds, God too responds, and a reciprocal or dialogic encounter is then in progress (cf. Jer. 11, 12). If man fails to respond to the divine initiative, the dialogue will be cut off at the very beginning, though God was prepared to make known the mystery of his will. As we read in Proverbs 1:23 (NIV): "If you had responded to my rebuke, I would have poured out my heart to you and made my thoughts known to you."

In the divine-human encounter God is an object who is also a subject. He is a subject who makes himself an object for our understanding. The subject-object relationship is not transcended but transformed into an I-Thou relationship. Personal fellowship, rather than mystical absorption, characterizes the life of prayer. I vigorously affirm this against Tillich, who maintains that true prayer transcends the divine-human encounter because it supposedly involves participation in the undifferentiated unity behind the subject-object cleavage.

## APPROACHING THE THRONE OF GOD

God makes us covenant partners in the working out of his purposes in the world, and yet we are not equal partners. God is the senior partner and must therefore be approached in awe and reverence. He is Master as well as Friend, but he is Master before he is Friend. God spoke to Moses as a friend (Exod. 33:11) only after the burning bush experience in which Moses had to hide his face, for he was afraid to look at God (Exod. 3:6). Afterward, God spoke to Moses through a cloud, for no one can see the face of God and live (Exod. 33:20).

We must prepare ourselves to approach the throne of the presence of God, but we must never regard ourselves as worthy to be received into this presence. It is not our action in preparing ourselves, but God's action in revealing himself that is the key to Christian prayer. Barth rightly says, "When man's own action, whatever its pretence or form, is made into a condition with regard to fellowship with God, then the Holy Ghost has been forgotten, then sin will be done to overcome sin."[17]

We can approach the throne of God only on the basis of the righteousness of Christ communicated to us by the Holy Spirit. We are made able to hear the Word of God only through the action of the Spirit of God, and we can receive this Word only when empowered by the Spirit. Barth underlines the decisive role of the Spirit in this matter of coming into the presence of God: "The hearing of the Word of God the Creator, which makes human life to become Christian life, is not man's work, but God's: the Holy Ghost's work. Just as our spirit cannot produce the Word of God, so too, it cannot receive it."[18]

How should God be addressed in Christian prayer? I believe that for the English-speaking person, "Thou" and "You" are both permissible. I have a slight preference for "Thou" because this term combines intimacy and reverence. It preserves the sense of the numinous in God, his inviolable holiness and majesty. On the other hand, when "Thou" becomes formal, then "You," being more familiar, should be used. The danger in the use of "You" is that God too readily becomes an anthropomorphic deity, a being who is the superlative of human qualities, a "Man Upstairs." A leveling process widely pervasive in modern society tends to reduce God to the level of humanity. I forthrightly repudiate the church banners that carry the inscription "God Is Other People." There is a loss of reverence for God today even in conservative evangelical circles. We desperately need to recapture the sense of God's awesome splendor and holiness.

Whether we use "Thou" or "You" in our prayers, we must approach the throne of grace with piety and reverence. Piety is a synthesis of the love and fear of God. It connotes a horror of blasphemy, a respect for the name of God. The Reformers recommended the practice of kneeling before God in private prayer, but this goes against the grain of democratic ideology, which masks a new secular religion, the cult of radical egalitarianism. Leslie Dewart echoes the new mood: "I think that the Christian theism of the future might so conceive God as to find it possible to look back with amusement on the day when it was thought particularly appropriate that the believer should bend his knee in order to worship God."[19]

True prayer must be learned, even though it must at the same time be voluntary and spontaneous. Forsyth perceived that we learn to pray through praying. The disciples said to Jesus, "Lord, teach us to pray" (Luke 11:1). Paul realized that we never know fully how to pray as we ought (Rom. 8:26). According to Thomas à Kempis, "it is a great art to commune with God." Luther agreed:

> Murmuring with the mouth is easy, or looks easy. But to fill the words with the sincerity of the heart in diligent devotion, i.e., desire and faith, so that we seriously desire what the words contain and do not doubt that the prayer is heard, that is a great work in the sight of God.[20]

Methods in prayer are more akin to ritual and mystical prayer than to prophetic prayer. Yet the biblical Christian, too, can learn from methods so long as they are seen as only stepping stones to the conversation of the heart with God. Strategies for improving the life of devotion can be helpful, but the devotional life must not be reduced to such things. Prayer is not a human technique but an action of the Spirit by which we are led to give utterance to sighs and needs that reside in the deep recesses of our inner being. The utterance of prayer bursts through all forms and methods: it signifies a breakthrough into freedom from the confinements and prescriptions of ceremonial law. Just as the Holy Spirit cannot be put in a box, so the life of prayer cannot be contained within the requirements of religious decorum. Yet those who are babes in Christ, those who are weak in the faith, need guidelines in order to grow in the life of prayer. Such guidelines, however, must never be made into hard and fast rules or laws. Each person will be led to develop his or her own methods in cultivating a life of prayer, since God addresses each person in a different way. Because God respects our individuality and seeks to meet us on the level of our understanding and spiritual progress, there can be no rules in the prayer life that are unconditionally or universally applicable.

True prayer is a dialogue made possible by the mediation and intercession of Jesus Christ. A Mediator stands between God and man. He prays for us and with us. His life is our model in prayer, and his Spirit is our instructor in prayer. When we look to Jesus and seek to give him the glory, his Spirit works in and through us enabling us to bring our requests into the presence of God the Father.

To whom should we pray? The church has always taught that prayers can be addressed to Jesus Christ and to the Holy Spirit as well as to God the Father. Because, as the Athanasian Creed expresses it, all three persons of the Trinity are equally God, we can come with our requests into the presence of each person. Prayers can also, of course, be addressed to the Trinity or Triune Godhead.

We may pray even to Jesus, since he is truly God as well as truly man. I assert this against Origen and Tillich, who advocated prayer only to God in himself. Origen held that Christian prayer, though offered through the Son, should be directed solely to the Father. In my estimation this betrays a false subordinationism which portrays only the Father as without origin and therefore the Logos or Son as less than the Father. Tillich is unable to affirm the full deity of Jesus Christ, since the object of his faith is the New Being that appeared in Jesus, not the pre-existent Word that assumed human flesh.

## TIME AND LENGTH OF PRAYER

The Bible does not prescribe the time or length of prayer, but it does offer guidelines. In Psalm 88 prayer is offered in the early morning (v. 13), and in Psalm 55 prayers are said evening, morning and noon (v. 17). The author of Psalm 119 advocates prayer seven times a day (v. 164). Daniel knelt for devotions three times a day (Dan. 6:10). Jesus prayed before sunrise (Mark 1:35) and in the evening when the day's work was over (Mark 6:46). Peter prayed at the third, sixth, and ninth hours.

Despite their aversion to prescribed formulas in the life of prayer that function as a new law, the Reformers did make general recommendations. On the basis of the Scriptural testimony Luther suggested that prayer should be "the first business of the morning and the last at night."[21] He advised: "Cultivate the habit of falling asleep with the Lord's Prayer on your lips every evening when you go to bed and again every morning when you get up. And if occasion, place, and time permit, pray before you do anything else."[22] Calvin urged that we offer prayer "when we arise in the morning, before we begin daily work, when we sit down to a meal, when by God's blessing we have eaten, when we are getting ready to retire."[23]

Just as the Christian is not bound to ritual laws that regulate the preparation for prayer, so he is not absolutely bound to set times for prayer. Yet there are times that are more appropriate for prayer than others: the gathering together for worship, the hours before work and bedtime, the time right before meals, when we need to remind ourselves of the goodness of God. But a Christian should feel free to pray anywhere, anytime, in the midst of daily work and play as well as in the solitude of his room in the early morning or late in the evening.

Concerning the length of our prayers, the saints through the ages generally advocated short prayers rather than lengthy ones. Jesus, who alone embodied perfect holiness, gave this warning: "When you pray, do not use a lot of meaningless words, as the pagans do, who think that God will hear them because their prayers are long" (Matt. 6:7, GNB). In this same spirit, Benedict of Nursia declared,

> We may know for certain that we shall be heard, not because we use many words, but on account of the purity of our hearts and our tears of sorrow. Our prayer, therefore, should be short and pure, unless by some inspiration of divine grace it be prolonged.[24]

For Augustine, the time of our prayer may be extended provided that we can afford to neglect other obligations and that this time is not filled up with many words. Prayer is to be "free of much speaking, but not of much entreaty, if the fervor and attention persist."[25] His preference was for the "very brief, quickly despatched prayers" that characterized the spirituality of the desert fathers.[26]

Continuing in this same tradition, Thomas Aquinas held that frequency, not length, is the important issue in prayer. Frequent short prayers are of more worth than fewer lengthy prayers. Because earnestness and zeal are crucial, he believed that prayer should continue as long as fervor is aroused, and it should end when weariness sets in.[27]

Luther recommended that our prayer times be numerous but short in duration. He lamented that "our prayer today occurs solely in the mumbling of the appointed hours, the counting of the beads of the rosary, and the babbling of words of that kind."[28] Those who wish to pray properly should say "brief prayers" that are "pregnant with spirit, strongly fortified by faith."[29] The people of God will pray constantly but always with few words and profound meanings. "The fewer the words," Luther declared, "the better the prayer. The more words, the worse the prayer. Few words and much meaning is Christian. Many words and little meaning is pagan."[30] The Lutheran mystic, Jacob Boehme, gave similar advice: "Many words are not needed, but only a believing, repentant soul that gives itself up with all earnestness into the mercy of God and God's comfort."[31]

Dwight L. Moody advocated short public prayers, though he acknowledged the need for constant prayer in the privacy of one's heart. "A man who prays much in private," he said, "will make short prayers in public."[32] Moody regarded lengthy public prayers as something akin to religious pretension.

Lengthy prayers are not to be ruled out altogether in the Christian life, but they should be considered more the exception than the rule. Many of the great saints spent hours in deep and fervent prayer and in reverent reflection on God's Word. Jesus passed whole nights in prayer and meditation. David fasted and prayed for one week (2 Sam. 12:16–23). Charles Simeon devoted four hours a day to prayer and Luther at least three. It is said of Francis of Assisi that he prayed so much that *"he became prayer."*[33] What characterized the great saints was not so much involvement in one single protracted prayer or the endless repetition of prayer formulas as the practice of constantly waiting on the Lord, of praying inwardly even when outwardly occupied in daily tasks.

The usual advice is to pray as long as one needs or wants to. Yet we should aim for conciseness in our prayers. We should put meaning into our words and avoid vain repetition. When prayer does not come easily to us, we should still make the effort to pray, whether we "feel like it or not." It is salutary to cultivate the habit of prayer. I concur with the counsel given in Georges Bernanos' *Diary of a Country Priest:* "If you can't pray—at least *say* your prayers!"[34] This is not Christian prayer at its best, but true prayer may arise out of it.

One can prepare for prayer by devotional reading and meditation. In the Old Testament, the recollection of the past acts of deliverance that God wrought for his people often served as a basis for prayer (cf. Deut. 9:25–29; 26:5–11; 4:9 ff.; 7:17–19; 8:2; 1 Kings 3:3–14; Gen. 32:9–12; Exod. 32:13). The memory of these events was to be stored in the heart to facilitate proper prayer. Solomon's humble prayer at Gibeon comes at the end of a preamble which is a recollection of God's grace, thus supplying a ground for the petition (1 Kings 3:3–14); the preamble in this case is part of the prayer.

Yet devotional reading, recollection, meditation—none of these should be seen as a substitute for prayer. Nor should we regard these things as prayer (unless they are included in our petition), since true prayer is dialogue with God. On the other hand, when meditation or reflection becomes listening to God's Word, it can then be seen as one stage in prayer. It nonetheless remains incomplete unless it is fulfilled in conversation.

Our whole life should reflect an attitude of openness to God, a sense of his abiding presence, and this is what is meant by Paul's recommendation to "pray without ceasing" (1 Thess. 5:17, KJV). Certainly such an attitude of prayerfulness will often give rise to silent intercession and supplication. This note can clearly be detected in Paul, who was constantly interceding for his fellow believers (1 Thess. 2:13; 2 Thess. 1:11; Rom. 1:9). It is also strikingly apparent in Luther:

> There is no Christian who does not have time to pray without ceasing. But I mean the spiritual praying, that is: no one is so heavily burdened with his labor, but that if he will he can, while working, speak with God in his heart, lay before Him his need and that of other men, ask for help, make petition, and in all this exercise and strengthen his faith.[35]

## WAITING AND STRIVING IN PRAYER

Prayer entails both waiting on God and striving to make our needs and requests known to him. Before we make meaningful petitions, we should pray that the Spirit might lead us in our prayer. We must wait in silence for his Spirit to come to us and work within us. "Wait for the Lord," says the psalmist, "be strong, and let your heart take courage; yea, wait for the Lord!" (Ps. 27:14). Following our petitions, we should then look forward in anticipation to God's answer: "Morning by morning I lay my requests before you and wait in expectation" (Ps. 5:3, NIV).

Dialogue should occur not just at the beginning but throughout our prayer. We should take the time to pause in prayer so that we can hear God's response and receive further guidance from his Spirit. There is waiting within prayer, as well as before and after prayer. It was Jacob Boehme's experience that after one beseeches God, "he will immediately hear in his soul that God will come to him in His grace, and give him in his soul the grace that He offered in Jesus Christ." [36] For Kierkegaard, "the true relation in prayer is not when God hears what is prayed for, but when *the person praying* continues to pray until he is *the one who hears,* who hears what God wills." [37]

The modern understanding is that "if you speak to God, that's prayer; if God speaks to you, that's schizophrenia." We need to recognize that, on the contrary, prayer is a personal encounter that entails a two-way conversation. God does not generally speak to his people in dreams and visions, though he sometimes speaks in this way. On the whole, the divine communication to humanity is a mystical one that transcends the senses and the imagination. Luther expressed it well: "I do not know it and do not understand it, but sounding from above and ringing in my ears I hear what is beyond the thought of man." [38]

God also speaks to us in the Bible and the sermon. He speaks in and through human words as well as deeds of kindness and mercy. Yet only the ears of faith can hear his Word, only the eyes of faith can discern his works. God remains the hidden God (*deus absconditus*) even in his revelation. There is no direct vision of God in this life, nor is there a direct communication with him that bypasses his Word, Jesus Christ.

I take issue with some charismatics who maintain that "when we speak in tongues, we communicate directly from our spirit to God." [39] It is presumed that praying with the understanding apart from the spirit is merely an indirect communication with God. We need to remind ourselves that God comes to us only through the medium of the human word or sacramental sign, and speaking in tongues is no less a human medium than the language of the intellect. We have no direct pipeline to God, but we do have the earthen vessel of the preached gospel, the words of the Bible, and the visible signs that compose the sacraments, and it is through these that we meet God and come to know his will and purpose for the world.

To be sure, everyone has a sense of the immediate presence of God, since God encounters every person through conscience and the works of nature. Yet God is experienced in this way as wrath and judgment. In order to know God as merciful and loving, we must be acquainted with his redemptive act in Jesus Christ, and this means that we can approach him in prayer only through Christ, the one Mediator between God and humanity.

There will always be a boundary between the Creator and the creature, not only in this life but also in the life to come. Even as his acknowledged sons and daughters we must not presume that we are on his level, that we can ever attain his status. This is why it is incumbent on us to worship and adore him even in the paradise of the blessed, even in the new heaven-earth; indeed, we shall then be ever more cognizant of what we owe him, of the depth and wonder of his grace and providence.

Prophetic religion seeks to maintain the discontinuity between God and humankind, because only in this way can we really pray with power and conviction. Only when we acknowledge our helplessness and sinfulness can we approach the throne of God as penitents, imploring his grace and mercy. Christ overcomes the estrangement between God and man, but he does not abrogate our humanity or creatureliness. On the contrary, he gives his people a heightened awareness of the great gulf that separates them from the holy God. Christ bridges the gulf between God and humanity, but he does not remove this gulf (as in some types of mysticism). The biblical Christian acknowledges that "God is in heaven and you are on earth" (Eccles. 5:2, NIV); this is why God must always be approached with deep-felt awe and reverence (cf. Isa. 6:5; 66:2). At the same time, we can come before the throne of grace in joy and confidence as well, knowing that our sins are covered by the righteousness of Christ, that our debts have been paid by the blood of Christ, that we now have an advocate and intercessor in the person of Christ. The one who believes is not reduced to nothingness by the grace of God but is now elevated to the status of a covenant partner with God. This is why we can pray to be made instruments of the will and purpose of God, agents in the winning of souls and the advancement of the kingdom of God on earth.

## NOTES

1. In W. Stanford Reid, *Trumpeter of God* (New York: Scribner's, 1974), p. 82.
2. John Calvin, *Institutes of the Christian Religion* Vol. II Trans. John Allen (Philadelphia: Presbyterian Board of Christian Education, 1936), III, 20, 16, p. 117.
3. Friedrich Heiler, *Prayer*, trans. and ed. Samuel McComb (New York: Oxford University Press, 1958), p. 362.
4. Jacob Boehme, *Jacob Boehme—The Way to Christ* (1623), trans. Peter Erb (New York: Paulist Press, 1978), p. 79.
5. Glossolalia in the context of prophetic prayer indicates a prerational form of prayer that nonetheless seeks rational elucidation. It does not cancel out the rational, as in the glossolalia of the mystery religions of the ancient Hellenistic world.
6. Martin Luther, *Luther's Works*, Vol. 6, ed. Jaroslav Pelikan (St. Louis: Concordia, 1970), p. 156.
7. Heiler, *Prayer*, p. 239.
8. Karl Barth, *Church Dogmatics: Index Volume with Aids for the Preacher*, ed. G. W. Bromiley and T. F. Torrance (Edinburgh: Clark, 1977), p. 414.
9. See Eddie Ensley, *Sounds of Wonder: A Popular History of Speaking in Tongues in the Catholic Tradition* (New York: Paulist Press, 1977).
10. Jacques Ellul, *Prayer and Modern Man*, trans. C. Edward Hopkin (New York: Seabury Press, 1970), p. 133.
11. Cited in Marcus Bach, *The Inner Ecstasy* (Cleveland: World, 1969), p. 149. Cf. Plato: "No man achieves true and inspired divination when in his rational mind." *Timaeus*, in R. G. Bury, trans., *Plato* (Cambridge, Mass.: Harvard University Press, 1961), Vol. 7, p. 187.
12. Boehme, *Jacob Boehme—The Way to Christ*, pp. 79, 80.
13. Dietrich Bonhoeffer, *Life Together*, trans. John W. Doberstein (New York: Harper, 1954), p. 79.
14. Amy Carmichael, *Thou Givest ... They Gather* (London: Lutterworth Press, 1959), p. 43.

15. Barth, *Church Dogmatics,* III, 3, p. 270.
16. Alfred de Quervain, *Das Gebet* (Zollikon-Zürich: Evangelischer Verlag, 1948), p. 21.
17. Karl Barth, *The Holy Ghost and the Christian Life,* trans. R. Birch Hoyle (London: Muller, 1938), p. 30.
18. *Ibid.,* p. 24.
19. Leslie Dewart, *The Future of Belief* (New York: Herder & Herder, 1966), pp. 203, 204.
20. Martin Luther, *D. Martin Luthers Werke* (Weimar Gesammtausgabe, 1888), 6: 2, 235. Cited by Regin Prenter in Marina Chavchavadze, ed. *Man's Concern with Holiness* (London: Hodder & Stoughton, 1970), p. 143.
21. *Luther's Works,* Vol. 43., ed. Gustav K. Wiencke (Philadelphia: Fortress Press, 1968), p. 193.
22. *Luther's Works,* Vol. 24, ed. J. Pelikan (St. Louis: Concordia, 1961), p. 387.
23. John Calvin, *Institutes of the Christian Religion,* ed. John T. McNeill, Vol. II, 3, 20, 50, pp. 917, 918.
24. St. Benedict, *The Rule of Saint Benedict,* ed. and trans. Cardinal Gasquet (New York: Cooper Square Publishers, 1966), p. 51.
25. *Saint Augustine: Letters,* trans. Sister Wilfrid Parsons, in *The Fathers of the Church,* ed. Roy Joseph Deferrari et al. (New York: Fathers of the Church, 1953), Vol. 18, p. 391.
26. In Joseph A. Jungmann, *Christian Prayer Through the Centuries,* trans. John Coyne (New York: Paulist Press, 1978), p. 36.
27. Thomas Aquinas, *Summa Theologica* II-II, q. 83, a. 14.
28. *Luther's Works,* Vol. 52, ed. Hans J. Hillerbrand (Philadelphia: Fortress Press, 1974), p. 139.
29. *Luther's Works,* Vol. 30, ed. J. Pelikan (St. Louis: Concordia, 1967), p. 322; Vol. 16 (Concordia, 1969), p. 320. Cf. Calvin: "We must not hope to obtain answers to our prayers to God by ceremonies, or . . . by making long prayers and great circumlocutions"—*Sermons on the Epistle to the Ephesians* (Edinburgh: Banner of Truth Trust, 1975), p. 680.
30. Quoted in Gerhard Ebeling, *On Prayer,* trans. James Leitch (Philadelphia: Fortress Press, 1966), p. 47.
31. Boehme, *Jacob Boehme—The Way to Christ,* pp. 80, 81.
32. Cited in *Christianity Today,* 19, no. 6 (December 20, 1974), p. 5.
33. Heiler, *Prayer,* p. 107.
34. Georges Bernanos, *Diary of a Country Priest* (London: Collins, 1956), p. 172.
35. Hugh Thomson Kerr, Jr., ed., *A Compend of Luther's Theology* (Philadelphia: Westminster Press, 1943), p. 109.
36. Boehme, *Jacob Boehme—The Way to Christ,* p. 75.
37. Søren Kierkegaard, *Journals,* ed. and trans. Alexander Dru (London: Oxford University Press, 1951) 572, p. 154.
38. Cited in Karl Barth, *The Word of God and the Word of Man,* trans. Douglas Horton (New York: Harper & Row, 1957), p. 179.
39. Merlin R. Carothers, *Power in Praise* (Plainfield, N.J.: Logos International, 1971), p. 53.

# V

# Heartfelt Supplication

## THE ESSENCE OF PRAYER

The essence of true prayer is heartfelt supplication, bringing before God one's innermost needs and requests in the confident expectation that God will hear and answer.[1] In the Old Testament this kind of prayer is described as the outpouring of the soul and crying to God out of the depths. In the words of the psalmist: "I pour out my complaint before him, I tell my trouble before him" (Ps. 142:2). And again: "O Lord, my God, I call for help by day; I cry out in the night before thee. Let my prayer come before thee, incline thy ear to my cry" (Ps. 88:1, 2). Another spiritual writer advises, "Arise, cry out in the night. . . . Pour out your heart like water before the presence of the Lord!" (Lam. 2:19). This same note is discernible in the book of Jonah: "In my distress, O Lord, I called to you, and you answered me. From deep in the world of the dead I cried for help, and you heard me" (Jon. 2:2, GNB). The association of prayer and the experience of despair is also noticeable in Isaiah: "O Lord, in distress they sought thee, they poured out a prayer when thy chastening was upon them" (Isa. 26:16).

Although the tendency to formalism and ritualism was more pronounced in later Judaism, spontaneous outbursts of praise and supplication were still very much in evidence. In the apocryphal book of Sirach we read: "He will set his heart to rise early to seek the Lord who made him, and will make supplication before the Most High; he will open his mouth in prayer and make supplication for his sins" (39:5).

Turning to the New Testament, we again see the emphasis on heartfelt supplication. Jesus told his disciples: "Ask, and it will be given you; seek, and you will find; knock, and it will be opened to you. For every one who asks receives, and he who seeks finds, and to him who knocks it will be opened" (Matt. 7:7, 8). In his own prayer life Jesus "offered up prayers and supplications, with loud cries and tears" (Heb. 5:7). Paul urged the Philippians: "Have no anxiety about anything, but in everything by prayer and supplication with thanksgiving let your requests be made known to God" (Phil. 4:6).

With the rise of a mystical spirituality that drew heavily on Neo-Platonism, petitionary prayer was considered on a lower scale than contemplative prayer, and in some circles the goal in the spiritual life was to transcend supplication altogether. Nonetheless, biblical motifs constantly resurfaced even among those who gave priority to contemplation. Despite his reservations on certain kinds of petitionary prayer, Augustine in his sermons recommends the prayer of "crying out" as the best way to meet temptation: "How deep in the deep are they who do not cry out of the deep."[2]

The Protestant Reformation signaled the rediscovery of biblical, prophetic prayer with its emphasis on supplication and intercession. For Luther, the most powerful prayer is "prayed with sobs and tears."[3] Because God is at the same time almighty and compassionate, he desires to hear supplications from his children. As Luther put it, "The Lord is great and high, and therefore He wants great things to be sought from Him and is willing to bestow them so that His almighty power might be shown forth."[4]

Among those on the modern scene who have seen the value of the biblical emphasis on supplication is H. H. Farmer:

Prayer . . . must have act and will at the centre of it, must be more than a mere state of mind, if it is to be the relation of a self to God, i.e., a genuine personal relationship. The expression of such act and will, such selfhood even in the very presence of the Eternal, is petition.[5]

## OTHER ELEMENTS IN TRUE PRAYER

Besides petition there are other elements in true prayer: adoration, thanksgiving, and confession. Yet it can be shown that there is present in all these the element of petitionary prayer. This is because all these forms of prayer spring from human need and seek an answer to human need. The integral relation of the various facets of prayer is admirably brought out in this definition from the Westminster Shorter Catechism: "Prayer is an offering up of our desires unto God, for things agreeable to his will, in the name of Christ, with confession of our sins, and thankful acknowledgment of his mercies."[6]

Certainly adoration and thanksgiving are both necessary for prayer to be fully Christian. As the psalmist expresses it: "Let all the joys of the godly well up in praise to the Lord, for it is right to praise him" (Ps. 33:1, LB). If prayer remains exclusively petitionary, then it is indistinguishable from the egocentric prayer of primitive religion, in which one is preoccupied with self rather than with the glory of God and the bounty of his mercy. Prayer becomes theocentric and Christocentric when our petitions are subordinated to the will of God and the advancement of Christ's kingdom.

Forsyth has aptly remarked that at the height of prayer and also at the beginning our attention should be focused on the great and glorious thing God has done for us in Jesus Christ. I would add that we should also gratefully acknowledge the goodness of God in creation and his loving, providential care. Adoration is inseparable from thanksgiving and indeed immediately erupts into thanksgiving (cf. Ps. 138).

For Richard Sibbes, praise and thanksgiving not only delight God but at the same time restore the soul:

> Praising of God may well be called incense, because, as it is sweet in itself, and sweet to God, so it sweetens all that comes from us. . . . We cannot love and joy in God but he will delight in us. When we neglect the praising of God, we lose both the comfort of God's love and our own too.[7]

However crucial in Christian prayer, adoration is nonetheless contingent on supplication. This is because only through the Spirit can we adore and give thanks. Adoration is a fruit of heartfelt supplication. To adore is to bring before God our sacrifices of praises and thanksgiving as suppliants. We present our sacrifices of praise for his acceptance. We approach the throne of God with the gifts that he has bestowed on us, but we ask him to accept these gifts, which are actually his own.

Just as praise and adoration are dependent on supplication, so they immediately give rise to new supplications. Sibbes makes this astute comment: "And upon offering this sacrifice of praise, the heart is further enlarged to pray for fresh blessings. We are never fitter to pray than after praise."[8]

Many of the great saints have argued that adoration is the highest kind of prayer. They have often pointed to John 16:23 where Jesus says to his disciples that on the day of resurrection they will ask nothing of him because their hearts will then be filled with joy. Yet Jesus returns to the subject of petition in the second part of verse 23: "If you ask anything of the Father, he will give it to you in my name." In verse 24 Jesus urges his disciples to ask, for then they "will receive" and their joy will be full. When we are united with the risen Christ in faith, we will ask no longer as beggars but now as sons and daughters. Even the saints in paradise who have entered into the glory of the coming redemption will continue to petition for their brethren on earth. So long as there is a relationship of dependence of the creature on the Creator, petition will figure prominently in the life of prayer; even when prayer takes the form of praise and adoration the petitionary element will nonetheless be present.

While praise and thanksgiving contain within themselves a petitionary dimension, petition in the narrow sense needs always to be informed by the motivation to extol and magnify the name of God and to give thanks for his great goodness toward us. Paul made clear the right motivation in our prayers in his epistle to the Philippians: "In all your prayers ask God for what you need, always asking him with a thankful heart" (Phil. 4:6, GNB).

The prayer of confession is even more indissolubly tied to petition than are praise and adoration. When we confess our sins, we ask the Lord to hear our confession and to grant us his forgiveness. In Isaiah 6 prayer begins with an invocation followed by a confession of sins and culminates in an act of dedication. In true prayer we go out of ourselves in praise to God. But we also go into ourselves in revealing our deepest needs and desires to God. Our deepest need is always for his grace and forgiveness.

Just as the soul of confession is heartfelt petition, so the whole life of prayer gains power and direction when anchored in confession. Oswald Sanders observes, "Until known sin is judged and renounced, we pray and plead in vain."[9] Jesus demanded that one should first be reconciled with one's brother before bringing gifts to the altar (Matt. 5:23, 24; cf. Matt. 6:14, 15).

In all Christian prayer the overriding motivation is to glorify God and to discover his will for our lives. We glorify God by seeking to know his will, by beseeching him to disclose his will to us. We also glorify God when we seek his aid in order to accomplish his will.

The basic goal of the Christian is to be united with God's will and to be conformed to the image of his Son, but this does not rule out lesser goals and desires. Farmer aptly declares:

Petitionary prayer . . . if it is not to be an unreal, abstract thing, is bound to be continually expanding and contracting from the general desire to be surrendered to God's will and to be rich in Him, to the particular interests which fill the daily life and in the pursuit of which the larger ends of personality can alone be achieved.[10]

The Lord's Prayer is the model of true Christian prayer, and a close examination reveals that it is essentially petitionary in nature. "Hallowed be thy name" expresses both the adoration of a joyful heart and the petition of a humble soul. It could just as well be translated "May thy name be hallowed." All the other sayings in this prayer are ostensibly petitions with the exception of the last: "For thine is the kingdom, the power and the glory forever." Adoration is present both at the beginning and the end, but petition is present throughout the main body of the prayer.

At the same time, the Lord's Prayer does not give the green light to every kind of petition. It limits our petitions, for we are not to ask beyond the necessities of life: "Give us this day our daily bread." It nevertheless permits us to pray for anything that promotes the plan of salvation, that advances the kingdom of God. This is clearly the implication of the petitions: "Thy will be done"; "Thy kingdom come"; and "Deliver us from evil." The Lord's Prayer reveals to us the kinds of things we should pray for, and though the will of God and the coming of his kingdom always have priority, they do not exclude a concern for our own salvation as well as for the necessities of daily life.


## STRIVING WITH GOD

Prayer is not simply petition, but strenuous petition. It is not just passive surrender but active pleading with God. It involves not only submission to the will of God but seeking to change his will. It consists not merely in reflection on the promises of God but in taking hold of these promises (cf. Isa. 64:7).

It is often said by those who are attracted to mystical or to philosophical prayer that our petitions change our attitude toward God but that they have no real effect upon God, who is unchangeable and impassible. My contention is that prayer does effect a change in God's attitude toward us and in his dealings with us. Prayer is reciprocal: it has a definite impact on both of the parties involved.

That God permits prayer to exert an influence on him is attested throughout the Scriptures. God sent Jonah to warn the city of Nineveh of his impending judgment, but when the people of Nineveh repented of their sins and hoped for God's mercy, the hand of God's wrath was stayed. When God threatened to destroy the people of Israel because of their gross idolatry, Moses interceded on their behalf and thereby turned away God's fierce anger (Ps. 106:23). The people of Israel provoked the Lord again because of their idolatry, and a plague was sent upon them. But Phinehas "stood up and interposed, and the plague was stayed" (Ps. 106:30). Later, when God prepared a judgment of fire for the people of Israel, Amos interceded, and we read that "the Lord repented" of his decision to punish his chosen people (Amos 7:1–6). In this light we can understand Spurgeon's contention that "prayer is able to prevail with Heaven and bend omnipotence to its desires."[11]

Prayer in the sense of striving with God in order to alter his ways with his people is nonsense to the philosopher, who relegates such an understanding to primitive mythology. Rousseau echoed the views of many when he declared: "I bless God for his gifts, but I do not pray to him. Why should I ask him to change for me the course of things, to work miracles on my behalf? I who ought to love above all the order established by his wisdom and maintained by his providence."[12] Kant is equally disdainful of prayer in the Christian sense, regarding it as a "superstitious illusion . . . for it is no more than a *stated wish* directed to a Being who needs no such information regarding the inner disposition of the wisher; therefore nothing is accomplished by it, and it discharges none of the duties to which, as commands of God, we are obligated; hence God is not really served."[13]

Against the philosophical understanding of prayer Karl Barth insisted that real prayer presupposes a living God who hears and acts: "He is not deaf, he listens; more than that, he acts. He does not act in the same way whether we pray or not. Prayer exerts an influence upon God's action, even upon his existence. This is what the word 'answer,' means."[14]

Christian faith, to be sure, affirms the essential trustworthiness of God's declared will and purpose for the world: God cannot deny or contradict himself. Yet Scripture makes clear that God has chosen to work out his purposes in cooperation with his children. His ultimate will is inflexible, but the ways by which he seeks to implement this will are flexible. He does not change his final purpose, but he does alter his methods for realizing this purpose. He is unchangeable in his holiness and righteousness but changeable in the giving of his grace (Heiler). Prayer, as Fosdick has observed, cannot change God's intention, but it does change God's action. Admittedly "prayer cannot change God's purpose, but prayer can release it."[15] According to William Law prayer is a mighty instrument, "not for getting man's will done in heaven," but "for getting God's will done on earth."[16] His contention is that the way in which God implements his will is contingent on our prayers, and in this sense we can change God's will.

Cooperation with the will of God sometimes entails challenging his will, trying to find a better way in which God's will (and not our will) can be done. There are always several ways in which God's will can be implemented, and through prayer we seek to discover the best way.

In our striving with God in prayer, we do not defeat God. As we prevail, so does he. We prevail in and through God. By our prayers we can alter the way in which God realizes his plan, but God sanctions this alteration. Norman Grubb offers this interpretation of Exodus 32:32:

> Save them, or damn me with them! If I cannot go to heaven with them, I'll go to hell with them! God can never refuse a holy desperation like that. It changes His mind. Of course, it did, because it was always his mind to save them.[17]

The most authentic type of prayer is humble supplication, the pouring out of the heart before God. Such prayer reveals our absolute dependence on God, our total helplessness apart from God. It also attests the incontrovertible fact that only those who actively seek help from the living God, only those who cast themselves on his mercy, can be used by God as instruments of his redemptive will and purpose.

Unlike primitive prayer, Christian prayer arises out of love and not exclusively out of need, want or fear. It is made in confidence more than in desperation. Petition for the Christian is not simply pressure applied to God but "filial reciprocity" (Forsyth). According to Forsyth, "Prayer should rise more out of God's Word and concern for His kingdom than even out of our personal needs, trials, or desires."[18] In Christian prayer we are not simply "driven by need" but "kindled by grace."

In our petitions we may indeed pray for material blessings, but they must be subordinated to a spiritual purpose. Philosophers and mystics have often opposed asking for material things. Augustine declared, "Ask nothing of God, save God himself." I contend that we may pray for anything that is in keeping with our eternal destiny, even when it appears to be "contrary to nature." After all, Jesus Christ is Lord of nature, and is therefore free to act within and upon nature as well as against nature. Temporal things may be prayed for if they aid us in our holy vocation.

To cease asking is to cease to be grateful (Forsyth). No earthly father would be satisfied that his son or daughter should take everything and ask for nothing. It gladdens God when his children approach him as a heavenly father and confide in him their deepest needs and desires. Only in this way is true fellowship established between God and humanity.

We should pray for what we believe could be God's final will or at least in accord with his will. How does one determine what is God's will? Scripture is our final norm on this matter, but the historical commentary on Scripture, the witness of the church through the ages, can also be of immeasurable help.

On the basis of Scripture I affirm that the "give me" prayer should always be subordinated to the "make me" prayer. The prodigal son in Luke 15 first asked his father to give him a portion of the goods that were due him so that he could make his own way in the world (v.12). After he tried to make it on his own and failed, he returned to his father to plead: "Make me as one of thy hired servants" (Luke 15:19, kjv). We have been given the privilege of being able to ask our heavenly Father for the good things of life, but these things will bring us only misery unless we ask at the same time to be good stewards of what we receive from him. The goods of this world will prove to be obstacles to our spiritual growth unless we seek to use these things for God's glory and not to satisfy our inveterate desire to have a place in the sun.

True prayer involves not simply pleading with God but also wrestling with God in the darkness. Wrestling is not whining, for it springs from strength, not weakness. It means refusing to let go of God without a blessing; as Jacob wrestled with the angel of God (Gen. 32:24–30), so the Christian wrestles with his God in prayer. To be sure, we also wrestle with the powers of death and hell and with the law of sin within us. But at the same time we wrestle with God, as Job persisted in doing: "If he would slay me . . . I should still argue my cause to his face" (Job 13:15, neb). A similar attitude is reflected in Luther's version of Jeremiah 20:7: "O Lord, thou hast persuaded me against my will, thou art stronger than I." The Canaanite woman who implored Jesus to heal her daughter and who persisted even after he at first refused also exemplifies this theme of striving or wrestling with God (Matt. 15:21–28).

This same note can be detected in Kierkegaard: "The righteous man strives in prayer with God and conquers—in that God conquers."[19] We resist what may be only temporarily God's will so that his ultimate will might be brought to light. We wrestle with God in order to discover the fuller scope of his will, and our success in this endeavor is therefore also God's victory. God accomplishes his purposes through the striving and pleading of his children.

There is, of course, a difference between resisting and rejecting (Forsyth). We resist the way in which the Lord might implement his will. When we resist God's will, we may be resisting what God wills to be temporary and to be resisted. Moreover, we resist on the basis of God's promises and not because of selfish motivation. Our resistance is born out of love, not hostility.

Jesus in the Gcrden of Gethsemane exemplifies the man of prayer striving with God. His prayer was "not stoic resignation to the inescapable, but a profound acceptance of the 'ways of God that are not the ways of man.'"[20] He did not meekly submit, but pleaded for his life. He surrendered to the will of his Father only after striving to change this will.

It is well to bear in mind that our striving with God is made possible only because God first encounters us and seeks to make us instruments of the divine will and purpose (cf. Isa. 65:1; Rev. 3:20). We are able to wrestle with God because God chooses to wrestle with us. God also wrestles with the powers of darkness that are bent on enslaving mankind. Moreover, God even wrestles with himself, seeking to reconcile his holiness, which cannot tolerate sin, with his infinite love for a sinful human race. This living God who agonizes over humanity and who reaches out to humanity in its lostness is forever to be contrasted with the Eternal Rest of classical mysticism and the distant, detached God of deism. This kind of God, who pursues his people even into the darkness and who safeguards them from all disaster, is poignantly testified to by Martin Luther in his much loved hymn "Dear Christians, One and All":

> To me he said: "Stay close to me,
>   I am your rock and castle.
> Your ransom I myself will be;
>   For you I strive and wrestle;
> For I am yours, and you are mine,
> And where I am you may remain;
>   The foe shall not divide us."[21]

## PERSEVERANCE IN PRAYER

Christian prayer is characterized not only by striving but by persistent striving. In Jeremiah we read, "You will seek me, and you will find me because you will seek me with all your heart" (Jer. 29:13, GNB). Paul urged his hearers to "persevere in prayer, with mind awake and thankful heart" (Col. 4:2, NEB). He described one of the disciples as "labouring fervently" in prayer (Col. 4:12, KJV). The literal rendering of this is "struggling on behalf of you in prayers" (cf. Col. 2:1, NASB; Rom. 15:30). This note is also readily discernible in Luther: "We should never lose heart; but we should persist in praying, wishing, and seeking until hope and the awaited liberation appear."[22]

The prayer of faith is importunate, agonizing prayer. God gives his promises without regard to our merits, but these promises must be claimed in faith. It was "by faith" that the patriarchs "obtained promises" (Heb. 11:33, NASB). Importunate prayer is strikingly illustrated in the parable of the widow who bothered the judge until he finally vindicated her (Luke 18:1–8).

> For a while he refused; but afterward he said to himself, "Though I neither fear God nor regard man, yet because this widow bothers me, I will vindicate her, or she will wear me out by her continual coming. ..." And will not God vindicate his elect, who cry to him day and night? Will he delay long over them?

For philosophy, this kind of prayer is an affront to human dignity. Yet we are not free until we give up our dignity and self-will. I am thinking here of prideful dignity, which is simply a manifestation of our lust for power.

Importunity in prayer is also evident in the salvation-history before the advent of Christ. David prayed and fasted all night that his son might be cured, ceasing only when the verdict was finally given (2 Sam. 12:15–23). Daniel besought the Lord to have mercy on his people (Dan. 9:3). Ezra interceded for God's people with fasting and weeping (Ezra 10:1–15). The note of importunity is also discernible in the book of Sirach: "The prayer of the humble pierces the clouds, and he will not be consoled until it reaches the Lord; he will not desist until the Most High visits him" (35:17).

The lives of the great saints of the church also bear witness to the need for perseverance and importunity in prayer. St. Monica stormed heaven with her prayers and tears for the conversion of her then wayward son, Augustine. Avitus, bishop of Vienne in France (fifth to sixth centuries), advised: "You must clamour in the accents of supplication; and if while the danger increases He still remains deaf, you must knock with unsparing hands." [23] Luther boldly came to the throne of grace seeking healing for his friend Melanchthon:

> This time I besought the Almighty with great vigor. I attacked him with his own weapons, quoting from Scripture all the promises I could remember, that prayers should be granted, and said that he must grant my prayer, if I was henceforth to put faith in his promises.[24]

Forsyth was especially emphatic that importunity is the hallmark of realistic communication between God and man: "Lose the importunity of prayer, reduce it to soliloquy, or even to colloquy, with God, lose the real conflict of will and will, lose the habit of wrestling and the hope of prevailing with God, make it mere walking with God in friendly talk; and, precious as that is, yet you tend to lose the reality of prayer at last." [25]

Sometimes the prayer of faith involves defiance of God bordering on presumption. Moses complained, "O Lord, why hast thou done evil to this people? Why didst thou ever send me? For since I came to Pharaoh to speak in thy name, he has done evil to this people, and thou hast not delivered thy people at all" (Exod. 5:22, 23). Even more presumptuous is this plea of the psalmist: "O God, don't sit idly by, silent and inactive when we pray. Answer us! Deliver us!" (Ps. 83:1, LB). A similar note is discernible in Psalm 44:23–26:

> Rouse thyself! Why sleepest thou, O Lord?
> Awake! Do not cast us off for ever!

Why dost thou hide thy face?
Why dost thou forget our affliction and oppression?
For our soul is bowed down to the dust;
    our body cleaves to the ground.
Rise up, come to our help!

Mystical religion generally frowns on this kind of presumption in prayer, and yet the naive prayer of the Bible reappears in some of the great Christian mystics. St. Teresa of Avila complained, "I do not wonder, God, that you have so few friends from the way you treat them." Fénelon, whose mysticism bordered on quietism, advised, "If God bores you, tell him so."

Although Calvin underlined the importance of surrender and submission to God's will, he nonetheless emphasized the necessity for perseverance in our petitions: "We must repeat the same supplications not twice or three times only, but as often as we have need, a hundred and a thousand times. . . . We must never be weary in waiting for God's help."[26]

Boldness and presumption are especially noticeable in the prayer life of Martin Luther. In 1540 Luther received word that his good friend, Frederick Myconius, had become fatally ill and had not much time left to live. Luther wrote to him: "I command thee in the name of God to live because I still have need of thee in the work of reforming the church. . . . The Lord will never let me hear that thou art dead, but will permit thee to survive me. For this I am praying, this is my will, and may my will be done, because I seek only to glorify the name of God."[27] This story tells us that it is permissible to become bold and presumptuous in prayer when one has the proper motivation—to advance the kingdom of God to his greater glory.

The boldness with which the Christian goes to the throne of grace, it should be noted, is derived from God, not from self (cf. Heb. 10:19). Indeed, we cannot be bold in God unless we are at the same time emptied of self.[28] A Christian, "when he is driven out of all comforts below . . . can wrestle and strive with God by God's own strength, fight with him with his own weapons, and plead with God by his own arguments."[29]

Prayer, to be sure, involves submission to the will of God as well as importunity. Yet our prayers must end and not begin with "Thy will be done." Jesus surrendered in the Garden of Gethsemane only after much agonizing, striving, and pleading with his Father in heaven.

Against mysticism I affirm that the surrender to God signifies not complete renunciation but the leaving of the fulfillment of one's wish to the free judgment and discretion of God. We pray that God will help us as he sees fit and meet our needs as he understands them. The surrender in prayer is not so much servile submission as seeking to bring our will into accord with his will. It is willing with God and thereby aiding God's will, becoming one with his will.

God wishes us to strive with him before we submit because he wants to convince us. He desires to see how earnest we really are. He hides the full meaning of his will from us until we are ready to accept it. When we finally surrender, we triumph in that God triumphs.

## EVANGELICAL VERSUS MAGICAL PRAYER

Magic intrudes into the life of prayer when the petitioner seeks to control or manipulate the divine power. The temptation to have recourse to magic is especially acute in primitive and ritualistic religion, but it is also present in mystical and even prophetic religion. When prayer is reduced to techniques or formulas, a magical predisposition is already in evidence. In the magical world view, God is either an impersonal power that can be laid hold of by artful technique or a deus ex machina that is brought in as a last resort to solve a problem. The magician envisions a God who is there at our bidding, who can be turned on or off like an electric current.

The belief that the mere repetition of the name of Jesus or the Hail Mary or the Lord's Prayer has automatic efficacy is more akin to magic than to biblical faith. Prayer in the name of Jesus entails not the repetition of the name of Jesus but the acknowledgment of what the name stands for. The Lord's Prayer, to be sure, is the model for Christian prayer, but it was not intended as a prayer formula to be constantly recited. Jesus did not say, "Pray these precise words" but "Pray, then, in this way" (Matt. 6:9, NASB). According to Calvin, "the Lord's Prayer does not bind us to its form of words but to its content."[30] While I do not dispute the rightful place of this prayer in a formal service of worship, we must always resolve to put meaning into the words and not simply say or chant the words.

A magical outlook also prevails whenever we make a point of testing God, whenever we lay down conditions for affirming his reality or accepting his guidance. There is a difference between asking God for spiritual discernment so that we can see his signs and putting God to the test. Gideon tested God when he demanded particular signs as the condition for obeying the divine commandment. He first asked that the fleece of wool on the threshing floor be covered with dew even though the ground was dry, and when he rose the next morning he was able to wring enough dew from the fleece to fill a bowl with water (Judg. 6:36–38). Then he demanded another sign: that the fleece would be dry and that the ground would be covered with dew, and on that night his petition was granted. Yet Gideon was aware that he was provoking the anger of God by his request. He was able to gain victory over the Midianites only when he was divested of external supports: his army was reduced to 300 men, and the only weapons they were permitted by the Lord were torches, trumpets, and empty jars (Judg. 7).

The Bible warns against placing trust in signs. The mandate of the Lord is that we walk by faith, not by sight. To seek for signs is to try to dictate the way in which God answers. It is asking God to go contrary to his Word. People of faith plead with God and complain to him, but they do not try to control God (as in primitive religion). There is no magic in prophetic prayer. We try to persuade through our petitions, but we do not manipulate.

To ask for specific signs is to incur the divine displeasure. The people of Israel in the wilderness "tested God in their heart by demanding the food they craved" (Ps. 78:18). He gave them what they asked for, but "he slew the strongest of them, and laid low the picked men of Israel" (Ps. 78:31). Again the children of Israel "soon forgot his works; they did not wait for his counsel. But they had a wanton craving in the wilderness, and put God to the test in the desert; he gave them what they asked, but sent a wasting disease among them" (Ps. 106:13–15). In Luke 1:18–22 we read that Zechariah asked for a sign and was struck dumb.

Demanding signs from God as the condition of our faithfulness is inspired partly by doubt. Oswald Sanders astutely comments that God's response to Gideon's twice-repeated request was "a gracious concession to the feebleness of his faith rather than a reward for its strength."[31] Because we do not trust in the promises of God, we crave outside guarantees. Our dependence is partly on human ingenuity and not wholly on the Word of God. Calvin aptly remarked, "If you doubt, you do not pray." Instead of questioning what we know to be the clear counsel of God, we should delight in the Lord, and then he will grant us the desires of our heart. When we commit our way unto the Lord and "trust . . . in him . . . he shall bring it to pass" (Ps. 37:4, 5, KJV).

The presumption that springs from a living faith is radically different from the doubt that is inspired by a failing faith. We can be bold in our requests because we know that we have an Advocate with the Father and that we can enter into his presence as adopted sons or daughters. When we begin to doubt, we are no longer sure of our status as sons and daughters, we are no longer certain that the Word of God is true.

Though we should not demand from God signs of our own choosing, we should pray to be open to the signs that God is already working in our midst (cf. Isa. 38:7, 8; Phil. 1:28, NIV). In this light we can understand the request of the psalmist: "Show me a sign of thy favor" (Ps. 86:17; cf. Ps. 74:9). Here it is evident that he is simply asking for spiritual insight in order to discern the working of God. In Isaiah 7:10–14, God orders King Ahaz to ask for a sign, and the Lord gives him a sign despite the fact that he does not ask (cf. 1 Kings 13:3).

Magical practices are especially prominent in the area of spiritual healing. Handkerchiefs or scarves that are blessed by the faith healer are alleged to contain divine potency and therefore to be instrumental in healing. The practice of anointing with oil, even though it has a scriptural basis, can open the door to magic, especially if the anointing is seen as an automatic guarantee of health or success. Some believe that the mere repetition of certain prayer formulas or protracted prayer accompanied by fasting will effect miraculous cures. In magical healing trust is placed not in the power of God but in the power of faith or in the one who is praying.

This does not mean, however, that we should not pray for healing. James refers to the prayer of faith which is able to work miracles (James 5:15). We should never resign ourselves to sickness but instead try to overcome it through the grace of God. Acquiescence or resignation to the way things are as "the will of God" is closer to Stoicism than to Christianity (Richard Foster). Forsyth has argued that God ordained disease for the purpose of being resisted. Yet when we are healed, the credit should go to God, not to the manner of our praying. It is not our prayers but God who is working through them that restores the sick person to health and well-being.

Healing is a gift of God; it is not the automatic result of human technique, even if this goes under the name of prayer. In the prayer for healing we do not seek to manipulate the divine power; instead we relinquish the afflicted person into God's hands. Healing, if it is to be lasting, is brought about by the Spirit of God and not by the spiritual exercises of man. Between divine healing and magical healing there is an ineradicable gulf.

The mental healing practices in the cults of the new transcendentalism are closer to magical than to messianic healing, since the source of healing is seen to be the power of the mind rather than a living Savior. It is commonly supposed in those circles that positive thoughts or affirmations of divine truth in and of themselves can effect spiritual healing. This is not to deny the element of truth in the neo-transcendentalist movement, for it can be shown that our mental state does directly affect bodily health. Yet the kind of healing that results from edifying thoughts is not yet spiritual healing, since the latter pertains to the whole person. So long as people are not in a right relationship with God, they are not yet well, even though they may have experienced a physical or even an emotional healing.

That the ministry of healing is one of the untapped resources of the church is becoming increasingly evident. Because the mainline churches have been reluctant to accept the validity of the healing ministry, the small sects and cults have been quick to enter this vacuum and with much success.

The reality of spiritual healing has been attested to by Emily Gardiner Neal, who as a skeptical news reporter began investigating claims of divine healing and as a result was converted to the Christian faith:

> I have witnessed again and again our Lord's merciful response to mankind's age-old and despairing cry: "I believe; help Thou mine unbelief." It was a father bringing his sick child to Jesus for healing who first uttered those words. A compassionate God extended His healing hand then, and He is no less merciful today. . . .
>
> A year ago an anguished father, whose small son was suffering from an inoperable brain tumor turned to God, offering Him what he had of faith augmented by desire and hope. It was enough. Week after week prayers were offered for the child as he received the laying-on-of-hands. His condition steadily improved. A month ago the doctors who had said there was no hope pronounced him completely well.[32]

Many false ideas surround the ministry of healing. One misconception, sometimes promoted in Pentecostalism, is that the person who is not healed lacks sufficient faith. This may be true in some instances, but it is manifestly untrue in others. God delivers in sickness either by removing it or by granting the strength to bear it (Oswald Sanders). In Hebrews 11 we read that by faith some overcame and by faith others suffered (Heb. 11:32–40). Paul was given a thorn in the flesh, and this was not removed despite his entreaties, but he was granted the power to endure it (2 Cor. 12:7–9; cf. 1 Cor. 10:13). The prayer for healing if offered in sincere faith will be answered by God, but in his own way and time. God may well answer our prayer by saving our soul or by healing our emotions even though he may leave us in physical sickness for a time.

Besides the area of healing, magical practices also find a fertile ground in the universal concern for preservation against danger. Some are not satisfied with a petition to God but crave additional protection against the powers of darkness, both spiritual and temporal, and therefore resort to practices that smack of superstition. I am thinking here of crossing oneself before entering a house where temptation resides, wearing religious medallions to ensure safety, or dipping one's hands in holy water to ward off demons.

The right weapon in the battle with the demonic powers is the prayer of preservation by which we commit ourselves into the hands of the living God. Luther recommended this prayer as a way to combat the devil, terror, and sudden death. It may be offered before or during any crisis and before embarking on a journey. It is also appropriate before sleep at night when our subconscious and unconscious are particularly vulnerable to demonic incursion. Luther suggested that we pray on such occasions: "Shield us, Lord, with thy right arm. Save us from sin's dreadful harm." A petition for the protection of the angels of God also has biblical warrant (cf. Gen. 24:7; Num. 20:16; Pss. 34:7; 91:11, 12; 1 Kings 19:5–7; Isa. 63:9; Matt. 2:19, 20; 4:6, 11; Luke 4:10, 11; Acts 5:19; 27:23, 24).

## INTERCESSORY PRAYER

Besides simple petition and the prayer of preservation, supplication can take the form of intercession. The prophets and kings of Israel frequently pleaded for their people before God (Exod. 32:11–14; 1 Sam. 12:7 ff.; 2 Kings 19:14–19; 1 Chron. 21:16, 17; Lam. 5; Dan. 9:16). Paul urged the Ephesians to pray for the whole household of God (Eph. 6:18; cf. Rom. 1:9; Phil. 1:3, 4). In 1 Timothy Christians were enjoined to make intercessions for all people, including kings and emperors (1 Tim. 2:1, 2). Polycarp declared, "We pray for all saints; for kings and rulers; for our persecutors and for enemies of the Cross."[33] According to Spurgeon, intercession is the most acceptable of all supplications, the very fat of our sacrifice. On one occasion Augustine defined prayer as intercessory supplication: "Prayer is to intercede for the well-being of others before God." The prayer for the healing of the afflicted is one form of intercessory prayer (cf. Num. 12:13; Mark 7:24–30; Luke 7:1–10). Moreover, the prayer of preservation, when directed to the well-being of others, becomes intercession.

The power of prayer is nowhere more clearly manifest than in the intercessions of the faithful. Through the prayers of the church, people are healed, lives are transformed, nations are changed. Hannah Hurnard, a Quaker mystic, has called intercessors "God's transmitters," since through their prayers God acts and speaks. Prayer, she insists, releases the power of God, which is likened to electricity. In a similar manner, Hallesby describes prayer as "the conduit through which power from heaven is brought to earth."[34] Admittedly such views suggest on the surface a semi-magical outlook; nonetheless it is recognized that God acts only in his freedom, though it is held that he freely binds himself to the prayers of his people.

For Calvin, supplication is opening up the treasures that God has stored for us in heaven.[35] These include not only personal blessings but blessings for others as well. Indeed, no treasure is greater than souls for the kingdom of God. Calvin firmly believed that through the intercessions of the faithful the kingdom of God could be advanced in the world and the powers of darkness overthrown.

Sibbes also had a keen insight into the amazing efficacy of intercessory prayer. "What cannot prayer do," he asked, "when the people of God have their hearts quickened, and raised to pray? Prayer can open heaven. Prayer can open the womb. Prayer can open the prison, and strike off the fetters."[36] For him, intercession is especially effective when people of faith are united in prayer: "A few holy, gracious men, that have grace and credit in heaven above, they may move God to set all things in a blessed frame below."[37]

The Old Testament is very clear on the power of intercessory prayer. The prayers of Abraham for the people of Sodom (Gen. 18:23–33) and of Moses for Israel (Exod. 32:11–14) are classic models of intercession. Psalm 106 describes how one person can save a whole nation, and the two examples given are Moses and Phinehas, who through their intercessions for the people of Israel stayed the hand of a wrathful God. In 2 Samuel 24 we read how the Lord sent a pestilence upon Israel because of David's sin in taking a census of the people. Yet, through David's prayers on behalf of his people, the plague was stopped.

Intercession not only powerfully aids our fellow human beings, but it also revitalizes the spiritual life of the intercessor. William Law discovered that when we intercede for others "all little, ill-natured passions die away" and our "heart will grow great and generous."[38] The missionary Bible translator Henry Martyn observed that in times of dryness and nagging depression he had often found inward renewal in the act of praying for the conversion or sanctification of others. Corrie Ten Boom relates how fear suddenly seized her on a harrowing car ride through the California mountains. She was able to regain interior composure when she began praying for others, people with whom she had traveled, her companions in a German concentration camp, her school friends of years ago.[39]

How does one pray the prayer of intercession? Evangelical piety has generally advocated mentioning people by name and praying for solutions to specific needs in the world. The mystical tradition of the church, on the other hand, has contended that simply to visualize the afflicted person in the light of God's grace is sufficient for that person's deliverance. St. Cyprian advised: "To help another think of that one as though he were with you, standing by your side, or kneeling with you in spirit, before that God to whom you pray."

The Pietists recommended prayer lists to remind the petitioner of particular people in need of intercession. Charles Whiston, veteran Episcopal missionary to China, has disclosed to me that at one time his prayer list totaled 2,000 names; he kept these names on filing cards and went through them daily so that by the end of the week all those on the list were included in his intercessions.

It is important to remember that the intercessory prayer of many humble people nurtured in the churches of evangelical Pietism has been responsible for the great missionary outreach of Protestantism. While the Reformers stressed intercessory prayer, it was directed more to the reform of the church than the conversion of the world to Jesus Christ. Not until the advent of Pietism and Puritanism in the seventeenth century did foreign missions begin to flower within Protestantism. And behind this great missionary thrust were the intercessions of prayer warriors who in their prayers lifted the missionaries into the presence of God, calling them by name and enumerating their needs, sometimes in detail.

Intercessory prayer was said to be the key to the remarkable success of the China Inland Mission, at least in its early years. At a conference of its few members in China in 1886, it was agreed that the pressing need was for no less than 100 new missionaries. As they discussed this almost impossible challenge, one of them asked, "Is anything too hard for God?" The whole company then turned to earnest, passionate intercession. As they continued in prayer, the conviction seized them that their prayers would be answered affirmatively. The meeting ended in thanksgiving and praise for the hundred missionaries that God had promised to send. That very year there was a marked increase in the number of those who volunteered for service with the China Inland Mission, and before the year ended, 100 new missionaries were sent out. Other missionary societies testify to equally impressive "coincidences."[40]

It is fair to say that in the evangelical tradition intercession has occupied a more prominent position than in the circles of radical mysticism. Indeed, among some of the more avowedly Christian mystics it is held that in true prayer Christ moves ever more toward the center, and we move toward the circumference. In the view of prophetic prayer, on the contrary, our needs and our neighbor's needs remain central, but they are now seen in the light of God's will as revealed in Jesus Christ.

## EFFECTUAL PRAYER

Our prayers are effectual if we really want what we ask for and believe that God can and will give it to us. Our Lord assured us, "Whatever you ask in prayer, believe that you receive it, and you will" (Mark 11:24). And in the words of John: "This is the confidence which we have in him, that if we ask anything according to his will he hears us. And if we know that he hears us in whatever we ask, we know that we have obtained the requests made of him" (1 John 5:14, 15). True prayer is offered in the certainty that it will be heard. Once we have asked, we should then live as if we had received.

The Reformers were particularly adamant on the subject of certainty in the life of prayer. Only prayers made in the assurance of faith and hope will carry the power of the Holy Spirit. Calvin declared:

> If we would pray fruitfully, we ought ... to grasp with both hands this assurance of obtaining what we ask, which the Lord enjoins with his own voice, and all the saints teach by their example. For only that prayer is acceptable to God which is born ... out of such presumption of faith, and is grounded in unshaken assurance of hope.[41]

Once we have prayed the prayer of faith, we must be willing to do what the prayer would require of us if answered. We must count the cost before urging God to bring about changes in our lives or in the lives of others. If we pray for racial peace, we must be willing to be instruments of God's purposes in bringing about such peace. The person who prays this kind of prayer must be prepared to go out of his way to befriend the people who are the objects of his intercession. There is a danger in praying for certain spiritual gifts, because it means that we must then be willing to embark on the ministry for which the gifts equip us. If we pray for the gift of healing, we are then committed to giving our time and energy to the sick who need healing. Abraham Heschel has aptly remarked, "A man's prayer is answered only if he stakes his very life on it."[42]

Not only must we be willing to act if our prayer is answered, we must seek to bring about the answer even as we pray. We should not only make known to God the desires of our heart, but we should put legs under our prayers. We must pray as if everything depended on God, but we must work as if everything depended on ourselves (Loyola). According to Sibbes, "In prayer we tempt God, if we ask that which we labour not for. Our endeavour must second our devotion."[43]

The efficacy of our prayers is tied to the discretion of God. He will answer the prayers of the faithful, but he will answer in his own way and in his own time. He will often give us beyond what we ask for. As Luther phrased it, "We pray for silver, but God often gives us gold instead."

Yet God may also answer with a refusal. He will not reject our prayer, but he may well reject the way we wish our prayer to be answered. We must not insist on our solution after it becomes clear that God chooses to impose another solution. There is a time to resist and a time to submit. God may delay his answer in order to secure our humble dependence on him. We need to wait for the right time, which is known only to him. It was seven years before William Carey baptized his first convert in India, and it was likewise seven years before Henry Richards gained his first convert in the Congo.

It is well to recognize that there will always be a tension and sometimes a contradiction between our desires and God's will. The reason is that sin still darkens the minds even of believers, so that we do not always know or desire what is best for us. We want to be respectable sinners, whereas God wants us to be self-sacrificing saints. We pray to be secure in our sin, not to give glory to God. We want to be co-creators and co-redeemers, not servants of the King. Our goal is to be winners, not slaves of righteousness.

Besides the moral gulf between God and humanity, there is the ontological discontinuity. God is infinite, whereas we are finite; he is the creator, we are only creatures. This immeasurable gulf between God and man is vividly portrayed by the prophet Isaiah: "My thoughts are not your thoughts, neither are your ways my ways, says the Lord. For as the heavens are higher than the earth, so are my ways higher than your ways and my thoughts than your thoughts" (Isa. 55:8, 9).

As finite creatures, we are inevitably conditioned by the culture and history in which we live, and this too accounts for our inability at times to understand the will of God. As people who live in a democratic culture, we are accustomed to thinking of authority in terms of group or national consensus. But the kingdom of God is an absolute monarchy. In order to fathom the mystery of his will, we need to detach ourselves from our democratic milieu in order to grasp a radically different standard of authority.

Because God's ways are not our ways and his thoughts are not our thoughts, God's answer will usually be somewhat different from what we request. This is why Luther could say, "It is not a bad but a very good sign if the opposite of what we pray for appears to happen. Just as it is not a good sign if our prayers eventuate in the fulfillment of all we ask for."[44] Mary Magdalene de'Pazzi (d. 1607), an Italian Carmelite nun, sometimes rejoiced if her requests were not granted, for this meant that God's will, not her will, was being done.

The paradox of prayer that is not answered according to human expectation but that is fulfilled in the perspective of eternity is admirably set forth in the following poem:

> He asked for strength that he might achieve;
> he was made weak that he might obey.

He asked for health that he might do greater things;
  he was given infirmity that he might do better things.
He asked for riches that he might be happy;
  he was given poverty that he might be wise.
He asked for power that he might have the praise of men:
  he was given weakness that he might feel the need of God.
He asked for all things that he might enjoy life:
  he was given life that he might enjoy all things.
He has received nothing that he asked for, all that he hoped for.
His prayer is answered.[45]

In our prayers we will not always get what we expressly desire, but we will receive what we need.[46] God's ways remain hidden even when he accedes to our requests, even when he gives us the desires of our heart. The hiddenness of God in prayer is forcefully expressed by Luther: "We pray for salvation, and he places us under greater damnation in order thus to save us, and, in such a tempest, he hides his way of granting our prayers."[47] Similarly, Richard Sibbes observes that God sometimes "heals by not healing, and leaves infirmities to cure enormities."[48] God sometimes allows the bad to fall upon us in order to save us from the worse.

God hides himself from us even in his revelation because he wants us to walk by faith, not by sight. Even when he grants just what we ask for, this does not prove the merit of what we request nor does it prove the validity of our prayer or the vitality of our faith. The efficacy in prayer can be discerned only by the eyes of faith.

Petition is the heart of prayer, but our prayer life should not be exclusively petition. The petitionary element will always be present if we are really praying. At the height of prayer, said Forsyth, we should be preoccupied with the great work of redemption wrought in Christ, apart from its immediate and particular blessing to us. As he saw it, prayer that is only entreaty results in faith in prayer rather than trust in God. According to Forsyth, petitionary prayer "is purified by adoration, praise, and thanksgiving."[49] Similarly, Karl Barth declares that where thanksgiving, repentance, and adoration "are at work, each will in its own way contribute to the purity of our asking, to the ordering and cleansing of our privation and desire."[50] Effectual prayer has its immediate source in the presumption of faith, but its ultimate ground is the grateful awareness of what God has done for us in Jesus Christ.

Those who pray from the heart often go through much agony in their prayer, but they are never left in agony. The reward for praying in the Spirit is the peace that passes all understanding, the interior calm that external circumstances cannot affect. As Calvin put it, "By prayer we cast our cares upon God, that we may have peaceful and tranquil minds."[51] Interior peace should not be the ultimate goal of our prayers, but it is the inevitable fruit.

## NOTES

1. C. W. F. Smith reminds us that the Hebrew and Greek words that are generally employed for prayer in the Bible mean "to request" from God or "make a petition" to God. See his "Prayer," in *The Interpreter's Dictionary of the Bible*, Vol. 3 (Nashville: Abingdon, 1962), p. 858.
2. See *Saint Augustine: Sermons on the Liturgical Seasons*, trans. Sister Mary Sarah Muldowney (N.Y.: Fathers of the Church, Inc., 1959), pp. 85, 86.
3. *Luther's Works*, Vol. 7, ed. J. Pelikan (St. Louis: Concordia, 1965), p. 375.
4. *Luther's Works*, Vol. 6, ed. J. Pelikan (St. Louis: Concordia, 1970), p. 159.
5. Herbert H. Farmer, *The World and God* (London: Nisbet, 1936), p. 135.
6. The Westminster Shorter Catechism, Q. 98. In Philip Schaff, ed., *The Creeds of Christendom* (New York: Harper, 1919), Vol. 3, p. 698.
7. Richard Sibbes, *Complete Works*, Vol. 1, p. 253.
8. *Ibid.*, p. 288.
9. J. Oswald Sanders, *Prayer Power Unlimited* (Chicago: Moody Press, 1977), p. 90.
10. Farmer, *The World and God*, pp. 137, 138.
11. Cited in Friedrich Heiler, *Prayer*, trans. and ed. Samuel McComb (New York: Oxford University Press, 1958), p. 279.
12. Jean-Jacques Rousseau, *Émile*, Bk. 2, in *Oeuvres Complètes*, Vol. 4 (Paris: Baudouin Frères, 1826), p. 198.

13. Immanuel Kant, *Religion Within the Limits of Reason Alone,* trans. Theodore M. Greene and Hoyt H. Hudson (New York: Harper & Row, 1960), p. 183. The attitude of Rousseau and Kant is by no means atypical of the philosophical understanding of prayer as Heiler documents in his *Prayer,* pp. 87–103.
14. Karl Barth, *Prayer,* trans. Sara F. Terrien (Philadelphia: Westminster Press, 1952), p. 21.
15. Harry Emerson Fosdick, *The Meaning of Prayer* (New York: Association Press, 1916), p. 63.
16. For Law, the prayer that is effectual for accomplishing God's will is "Prayer in *the Name of Christ,* to which nothing is denied"—in William Law, *The Spirit of Prayer and the Spirit of Love,* ed. Sidney Spencer (*Canterbury*: Clarke, 1969), p. 120; cf. p. 55. Also cf. *The Works of the Reverend William Law,* Vol. 6 (Canterbury: Moreton, 1893), pp. 135–136.
17. Cited in DeVern Fromke, *Unto Full Stature* (Mt. Vernon, Mo.: Sure Foundation Publishers, 1965), p. 214.
18. P. T. Forsyth, *The Soul of Prayer,* 5th ed. (London: Independent Press, 1966), p. 79.
19. Søren Kierkegaard, *Edifying Discourses,* trans. David F. Swenson and Lillian Marvin Swenson (Minneapolis: Augsburg, 1946), Vol. 4, pp. 113 ff.
20. Nicholas Ayo, "At Night in Prayer," *The Christian Century,* 88, no. 51 (1971): 1496.
21. Martin Luther, "Dear Christians, One and All," in *Lutheran Book of Worship* (Minneapolis: Augsburg, 1978, 2nd printing), No. 299.
22. *Luther's Works,* Vol. 5, ed. J. Pelikan, p. 362.
23. In Herbert Thurston and Norah Leeson, eds., *The Lives of the Saints,* originally compiled by Alban Butler (London: Burns Oates & Washbourne, 1936), Vol. 5, pp. 127, 128.
24. Cited in Bengt R. Hoffman, *Luther and the Mystics* (Minneapolis: Augsburg, 1976), p. 196.
25. Forsyth, *The Soul of Prayer,* p. 92.
26. John Calvin, *Sermons on the Epistle to the Ephesians* (Edinburgh: Banner of Truth Trust, 1975), p. 683.
27. Cited in O. Hallesby, *Prayer,* trans. Clarence Carlsen (Minneapolis: Augsburg, 1931), p. 131.
28. See Sibbes, *Complete Works,* Vol. 1, p. 224.
29. Sibbes, *Complete Works,* Vol. 1, p. 198.
30. John Calvin, *Institutes of the Christian Religion,* Vol. II, ed. John T. McNeill, III, 20, 49, p. 917.
31. Sanders, *Prayer Power Unlimited,* p. 70.
32. Emily Gardiner Neal, *God Can Heal You Now* (Englewood Cliffs, N.J.: Prentice-Hall, 1958), pp. 29, 30.
33. Cited in Sanders, *Prayer Power Unlimited,* p. 102.
34. Hallesby, *Prayer,* p. 117.
35. In one of his sermons on Ephesians, Calvin likens the prayers that we offer to "keys by which to come to the treasures that God reserves for us and

which he will not keep from us. Therefore we must open the way to them by praying." In Calvin, *Sermons on the Epistle to the Ephesians,* p. 678.

36. Sibbes, *Complete Works,* Vol. 3, p. 186.
37. Sibbes, *Complete Works,* Vol. 6, p. 107.
38. William Law, *A Serious Call to a Devout and Holy Life,* ed. John W. Meister (Philadelphia: Westminster Press, 1955), p. 135.
39. Corrie Ten Boom, *Amazing Love* (New York: Harcourt Brace Jovanovich, 1977), pp. 52, 53.
40. See Albert D. Belden, *The Practice of Prayer,* (New York: Harper, n.d.), p. 39.
41. Calvin, *Institutes of the Christian Religion,* ed. John T. McNeill, III, 20, 12, p. 865.
42. Cited in Robert Raines, *The Secular Congregation* (New York: Harper & Row, 1968), p. 113.
43. Sibbes, *Complete Works,* Vol. 7, p. 204.
44. Martin Luther, *Lectures on Romans,* ed. and trans. Wilhelm Pauck (Philadelphia: Westminster Press, 1961), p. 240.
45. *The Paradox of Prayer* by Col. R. H. Fitzhugh. I first encountered this prayer at a Camps Farthest Out conference at Lake Koronis, Minnesota, in the summer of 1962.
46. Cf. Johann Arndt: "Where prayer is not answered according to our will, it is answered according to our needs: where it is not answered in a physical way, it is answered in a spiritual way"—Peter Erb, trans. and ed., *Johann Arndt: True Christianity* (New York: Paulist Press, 1979), p. 213.
47. *Luther, Lectures on Romans,* ed. Pauck, p. 246.
48. Sibbes, *Complete Works,* Vol. 7, p. 173.
49. Forsyth, *The Soul of Prayer,* p. 37.
50. Karl Barth, *Church Dogmatics: Index Volume with Aids for the Preacher,* ed. G. W. Bromiley and T. F. Torrance (Edinburgh: Clark, 1977), pp. 307, 308.
51. John Calvin, *Genesis,* trans. and ed. John King (Edinburgh: Banner of Truth Trust, 1975), Vol. 2, p. 193.

# Prayer and Mysticism

## CONFRONTING THE MYSTICS

The relationship between Christian prayer and mysticism has already been discussed, though not in depth. My aim in this chapter is to explore the mystical dimension in prayer as well as the divergences between what has come to be known as mystical prayer and biblical or prophetic prayer. It is my firm belief that these two types of prayer must be seen in the context of two disparate types of spirituality. I readily grant that there was an attempt at a synthesis of these two spiritual traditions in much of the piety of the early and medieval church, though the tension between them was never fully overcome. I also recognize that many of the great mystics of both Catholicism and Protestantism were devout and earnest students of the Scriptures and that their spirituality therefore reflects biblical as well as Platonic and Neo-Platonic themes.

While it is widely acknowledged that Christian mysticism is heavily dependent on the conceptual tools of Neo-Platonism in particular, some scholars are asking whether Neo-Platonism was simply a medium rather than the basis for the spirituality of the great Christian mystics, including Meister Eckhart and John Tauler. My position is that biblical faith was to some extent compromised in the thought of both these men, though this is much more apparent in Eckhart than in Tauler, whose spirituality had a formative influence on the young Luther.[1] This is not to deny the warm piety and sincere faith of both these towering figures of mysticism, nor is it to call into question the fact that both were believing and practicing Christians. Neither is it to deny that evangelical Christians can benefit in a positive way from a study of their writings as well as the works of many other great mystics of the church. It is indisputable that philosophical themes overshadow and even subvert biblical motifs in such noted representatives of modern mysticism as Gerald Heard, Alan Watts, Teilhard de Chardin, and Nikos Kazantzakis.[2]

It is my intention to demonstrate that these two strands of piety remain quite distinct, and this is especially evident in the way they understand prayer. I have no difficulty in acknowledging that prayer in its Christian sense contains a mystical element. In Christian prayer we are lifted above ourselves by the Spiritual Presence. At the same time, this should also be seen as an encounter with the divine person, Jesus Christ.

Christian prayer entails both external and internal relations. It is both an external act of communication and an inner act of communion (Nels Ferré). In the act of prayer we are related to the God who stands outside and above us but who also, by his Spirit, dwells within us. This inner or mystical dimension of Christian faith is apparent in these words of Paul: "Do you not realize that Jesus Christ is in you?" (2 Cor. 13:5), and "Christ in you, the hope of glory" (Col. 1:27). By the action of the Spirit, we are moved to petition the Father, and thereby we enter into a living communion with him. Yet the prayer of faith is not mystical prayer, just as the Christian faith is not mysticism.

## TWO PATTERNS OF SPIRITUALITY

In the phenomenology of Christian religion two distinct types of spirituality are discernible: biblical personalism and Christian mysticism. The former has its source in the prophetic tradition of biblical history; the latter signifies a synthesis of Christian and Neo-Platonic motifs, though it also draws from the Greek mystery religions and Oriental philosophy.[3]

In his book on prayer, Friedrich Heiler, as previously noted, draws a sharp distinction between prophetic and mystical religion, which is roughly analogous to my distinction.[4] He argues forcefully that these signify two radically different orientations toward God, man and the world. Prophetic religion is present among Jews and Moslems as well as among Christians, but its foremost representatives outside of biblical history are the Protestant Reformers, particularly Martin Luther. Heiler makes a convincing case that mysticism

> is neither a Christian inheritance nor a peculiarity of the Christian religion, although in this religion it has assumed its finest and most beautiful form. It has penetrated into Christianity (as also into Judaism and Islam) from the outside, from the syncretist mystery religions, later religious philosophy, especially from neo-Platonism. The Gnostics and the Alexandrians, but above all Augustine and the Areopagite, were the gates by which it entered. Mysticism has indeed lost in purity and logical quality, but has gained in depth and warmth, fervour and power, from an intermingling with prophetic religion.[5]

Among neo-orthodox theologians there was a marked aversion toward mysticism, and the contrast was often made between biblical and evangelical faith on the one hand and mystical spirituality on the other. According to Emil Brunner, mysticism dissolves the historicity of revelation: "In the idealist-mystic teaching, knowledge is neither revelation nor decision, but a perception of something that was always 'there,' ready to be perceived."[6] Hendrik Kraemer even argues that the mystical quest is rooted in human sin:

> The mystic who triumphantly realizes his essential oneness with God, or the World-Order, or the Divine, knowing himself in serene equanimity the supreme master of the universe and of his own destiny, and who by marvelous feats of moral self-restraint offers a fascinating example of splendid humanity . . . nevertheless, in the light of

Biblical revelation, commits in this sublime way the root-sin of mankind—"to be like God."[7]

Roman Catholic scholars not surprisingly have been much more reluctant to sound a warning against mysticism, although voices have been raised here and there against a too-ready equation of mysticism and Christianity. Baron Friedrich von Hügel contends that pure mysticism is none other than pantheism, "a non-moral, a supra-moral and a non-personalist position, within which there is really no place for a distinct and definite God."[8] Hans Küng contrasts the God of mysticism, which is essentially passive, with the God of the Bible, who is ever active, calling people to decision and obedience.[9] Although appreciating what is valid and helpful in the mystical tradition, Zaehner acknowledges that "the mainstream of Christian mysticism . . . is probably more influenced by Neo-Platonism and Pseudo-Dionysius . . . than it is by anything in the New Testament."[10] Thomas Molnar is quite emphatic in his criticisms of the mystical philosophical tradition and points to the contrast between the transcendent, personal God of biblical faith and the immanental God of mysticism.[11] Matthew Fox affirms a "creation-centered spirituality" over against what he terms a "neo-Platonic spirituality," and expresses his appreciation to the Protestant Reformers for reinstating biblical social prophecy.[12]

In delineating the two types of spirituality we should first recognize that in mysticism the emphasis is on the experience of unity with the divine presence, which is the ground of the self as well as of the world. Man is taken up beyond himself into a blissful union with the One or the Absolute or the World Soul. His spirit is absorbed into the Spirit of God (Tauler). He becomes one with the One in the All.

In the so-called evangelical experience or experience of encounter, the person of faith is conscious of his individuality, of the Creator-creature distinction. He is aware only of his unworthiness before God (Isa. 6), not of any essential unity with God.

The more intimate his communion with God, the more poignantly he senses the infinite distance between himself and God.

The hallmark of mystical religion is a direct experience of God apart from external mediation. In the words of Ruysbroeck: "The inward man performs his introspection simply . . . above all activity and . . . all virtues, through a simple inward gazing in the fruition of love. And here he meets God without intermediary."[13] "God," Eckhart declares, "acts without instrumentality and without ideas."[14] Schleiermacher views the mystical experience as "immediate self-consciousness."

Evangelical religion, on the other hand, emphasizes the need for a historical mediator between God and humankind, Jesus Christ. Calvin contended that "there is but one way by which to have good and infallible access to God, and that is by beholding him in his living image, for his majesty is too high, too much hidden, and too deep for us."[15]

Also crucial in this kind of spirituality is the pivotal role assigned to external means of grace such as the Bible and the sermon. Luther was adamant that "we must first hear the Word, and then afterwards the Holy Ghost works in our hearts; he works in the hearts of whom he will, and how he will, but never without the Word."[16] Some evangelical theologians such as Aulén and Turretin have held that God acts directly upon our hearts but always in conjunction with external means or aids.

In the deepest sense, the mystical experience is beyond the rational, beyond words and ideas. The mystic seeks to contemplate God in the obscurity of a blind faith, "void of all distinct and express images."[17] Thomas Merton asserts that "the mystical knowledge of God . . . is above concepts. It is a knowledge that registers itself in the soul passively *without an idea.*"[18] A medieval mystical writer gives this advice: "Reject all thoughts, be they good or evil."[19]

In biblical religion, on the contrary, faith includes the rational element. Faith goes beyond the humanly rational, but not be yond the Logos as in Neo-Platonism. Karl Barth even affirms that faith itself is a rational experience, since its object is a divine message as well as a divine presence.

Christian mysticism adopted Platonic and Neo-Platonic terminology to describe the mystic way of salvation: purgation, illumination, union, and ecstasy. Ecstasy is seen as the culminating point in the state of contemplative union. By contrast, the way of biblical faith entails repentance, assurance, and service. These stages may also be viewed as the awakening to faith, repentance, and obedience. Both Calvin and Luther saw the mystical union as being actualized in faith; purgation or repentance as well as works of love were believed to proceed from this union rather than prepare the way for it. For the biblical Christian, it is not the vision of God but the glorifying of God in the service of our fellow human beings that constitutes the goal of true religion.

In mysticism, on the other hand, the service of our neighbor is considered less important than service to the supreme object or highest good. We serve God in humanity rather than humanity as such. It is well to note Reinhold Niebuhr's strictures on Augustine at this point: "Augustine wants us to love the neighbor for the sake of God" and "to prove the genuineness of our love of God . . . by leading him [our neighbor] to God." Niebuhr also chides John of the Cross for regarding "the love of the creature as a ladder which might lead us to the love of God."[20]

Anders Nygren, in his noted *Agape and Eros,* manifests a similar reaction to Christian mysticism, which, he believes, is characterized by self-regarding rather than self-sacrificing love.[21] The *Caritas* of Augustine and Aquinas he views as an unwholesome synthesis between Agape and Eros, with the latter motif predominating. The love exalted by the mystics is interested not in serving the lowest but in aspiring to the highest—the fulfillment and perfection of self in union with God. Nygren is, in my opinion, unduly critical of mysticism, to the point of failing to make a place for the love directed to God; nonetheless, he reminds us of the incontestable gulf between Hellenistic spirituality, the primary source of Christian mysticism, and biblical piety.

Albrecht Ritschl's judgment on mysticism is equally harsh:

> Mysticism teaches escape from the world and renunciation of the world, and it places the significance of the ethically good action and the formation of virtues far beneath ecstatic union with God. Luther taught that the Christian religion leads to spiritual dominion over the world, and he placed the same value on the service of ethical action toward other men as on those activities which comprise man's reconciliation with God.[22]

It must be acknowledged that many mystics, perhaps reflecting their own immersion in the Bible, did not lose sight of the need for service to one's neighbor. Eckhart contended that if one is in contemplation and sees a person in dire need he should break off from contemplation in order to lend a helping hand. In her ecstatic vision, Catherine of Siena relayed these words of her Lord:

> It is impossible for you to give me the love that I ask, but I have given you a neighbor that you may do for him that which you cannot do for me. Love him without any worldly thought, without looking for any gain or return. That which you do for him, I look upon as done for me.[23]

This mystic is here describing Agape love, not even *Caritas* as defined by Nygren. Teresa of Avila expressed similar sentiments. Some of the mystics alluded to a state beyond spiritual marriage—spiritual fecundity, in which we share the fruits of our contemplation with those less fortunate. For such figures as Gregory the Great, however, the contemplative should regret the necessity of action, even when it is a matter of duty.

In this discussion it should be kept in mind that these two kinds of spirituality are ideal types, and finding exceptions to the rule does not impair the validity of the kind of distinction we are trying to make.[24] It should be noted, too, that even in those mystics who speak of spiritual fecundity, service of one's neighbor is still subordinated to the final goal of the blessed vision of God, ecstatic reunion with the Eternal. Nonetheless, authentic biblical and evangelical insights can be discerned again and again in the writings of many of the Christian mystics, and this is because they appeal to the Bible as well as to the mystical scheme of Neo-Platonic philosophy. In a great number of other mystics, however, including Christian mystics, the biblical personalist note is definitely muted, and what Söderblom calls "a mysticism of the infinite" reigns supreme.[25]

When we come to the doctrine of God, the cleavage between the two types of spirituality is especially noticeable. In prophetic religion, God is Personal Spirit, a divine Person who seeks fellowship with his children. In mysticism, God is a suprapersonal ground of being who is accessible to the creature only after the latter has climbed the mystical ladder of love to heaven. Radhakrishnan says that "the personal category is transcended in the highest experiences of the Christian mystics."[26] Mysticism has an affinity with pantheism and also with panentheism, in which the accent is on interdependence rather than identity; evangelicalism is correlative with biblical theism, which emphasizes the essential independence of the Creator from the creature. The Christian atheism of Thomas Altizer proves to be a kind of secular mysticism, as is also the case with the Jewish atheism of Richard Rubenstein, who refers to God as the "Holy Nothingness" out of which all things come and to which all things return.

Pantheistic and panentheistic themes are present in nearly all the Christian mystics, even in those who speak of a personal relationship with Jesus Christ. For Eckhart, the core of the soul is God. Teresa of Avila declared, "There is nothing in me that is not God: my 'me' is God." Catherine of Genoa went so far as to claim: "My being is God, not by simple participation but by a true transformation of my being."[27] Thomas Merton betrays a Platonic proclivity when he says that "the 'unreality' of material things is only relative to the greater reality of spiritual things."[28]

The God of mysticism reflects the feminine element in religion in that he is depicted as a passive Subject who moves the world by the lure of his all-surpassing perfection.[29] The God of prophetic religion, on the other hand, is the One who acts in history; he constantly intervenes in the world and moves it by the sheer force of his omnipotent power.[30]

Again, mystical religion is ahistorical in that it deemphasizes or obscures the historical particularity of the biblical revelation. Mystics the world over, both Christian and non-Christian, speak not of a divine incursion into human history but of the journey to the center, the divine core of the soul. In Meister Eckhart, the birth of the Son in the human soul is ranked above the historical incarnation in Jesus.

Mystics also refer to the need to look beyond the temporal to the Eternal. The inner light or the mystical experience is the primary criterion, not the Word of God. The Lutheran mystic Jacob Boehme declared, "The entire Bible lies in me." There is among Christian mystics an attempt to get beyond the historical Christ to God in himself. In the words of Augustine: "Were not the form of his humanity withdrawn from our bodily eyes, love for him in his Godhead would never cleave to our spiritual eyes."[31]

Prophetic or biblical religion is markedly historical. Revelation is said to take place in the events in the life of a particular people, the children of Israel, culminating in the personal history of Jesus Christ. The eschatological goal is not a timeless eternity but a new heaven and a new earth. The object of our hope is not escaping from time into eternity but the transformation of time by eternity. It is interesting to note that the renowned Jesuit scholar Karl Rahner, who tries to hold biblical and mystical motifs in balance and emphasizes the significance of the revelation in biblical history, can nevertheless remark: "Accomplished salvation is in no sense a moment in history but rather the culminating cessation of history."[32]

Equally striking are the disparate conceptions of evil in the two types of spirituality. Mystics are accustomed to speak of evil in terms of finitude, ignorance or weakness. It is traceable to a lack or deficiency within humanity, to nonbeing rather than to being. It is the "omission of good" (Dionysius) or a "defect" of the will (Augustine). In Buddhism sin is a "thirst for life."

For biblical, evangelical faith evil is not mere deficiency but positive rebellion. It is not natural desire but a lust for power. It signifies a perversity of the will, as Augustine also saw, and not simply moral weakness. It represents not merely the absence of good but an assault upon the good.

Pure mysticism is nonethical. The aim is to transcend the polarity between good and evil. The primal sin is individuation and the fundamental need reunion with the ground of being. This was certainly the stance of Neo-Platonism, though in Platonism the highest reality is the Idea of the Good, and not a few Christian mystics would here be closer to Plato than to Plotinus.

Biblical faith traces moral distinctions to the heart of God and sees sin as an affront to the holiness of God. The primal sin is rebellion against a holy God, and the fundamental need is divine forgiveness. God does not include all opposites within himself (as in monistic mysticism) but signifies a purity of love that excludes and judges evil.

With such widely differing concepts of evil, conflicting approaches to the doctrine of conversion are only to be expected. In pure mysticism, conversion means turning from the manifold to the essential. In biblical religion, it means turning from the way of sin to the way of righteousness. The experience of conversion is often portrayed as a shattering one in both types of spirituality, but whereas in biblical faith the emphasis is on conviction of sin, in mysticism the stress is on rapture and bliss.

The difference between the two spiritualities might be likened at this point to the tension between a theology of the cross (*theologia crucis*), which was especially pronounced in Luther, and a theology of glory (*theologia gloriae*). In the former we live under the cross and walk by faith waiting for the rapture of resurrection glory, while in the latter we can anticipate the glory of Eternity now in mystical experience and ecstasy. A *theologia gloriae* is reflected in Bernard of Clairvaux, who remarks that contemplation "sometimes for brief intervals holds the admiring soul aloft in stupor and ecstasy."[33] Yet the Christian mystics also stressed the life of faith and suffering, and some referred to "the dark night of the soul," in which the Christian is divested of external supports and securities and must cling to God only in faith.[34] At the same time, many of them affirmed the possibility of the beatific vision of God on this side of death.[35]

Still another area of divergence is the matter of relationship to the world. In mysticism holiness usually means retirement from the world, while in prophetic religion the emphasis is on mission to the world—even dominion over the world. The evangelical vision is to bring all peoples into submission to the Lordship of Jesus Christ, and this accounts for the attention given to world mission and evangelism. John Wesley gave voice to this concern when he claimed that he could change the world with only "one hundred preachers who fear nothing but sin and desire nothing but God . . . such alone will shake the gates of hell and set up the kingdom of heaven upon earth."[36]

Conversely, where mysticism is dominant the focus is on detachment from the world of the senses. Eckhart remarked, "I praise seclusion in preference to all love."[37] According to Thomas Aquinas, whose mystical temperament was not significantly altered by an evangelical thrust, "For a man to be open to divine things, he needs tranquility and peace."[38] Although he inadvertently became involved in the politics of his time, Bernard of Clairvaux nevertheless advised: "Sit alone, having nothing in common with the crowd, nothing with the multitude of the others. . . . Holy soul, remain alone, and keep yourself for him alone out of all the others."[39] In the words of Walter Hilton, "Whoever receives this gift of fervour from God should withdraw from the company of other people and be alone, so that it may not be interrupted."[40] Thomas à Kempis gave similar counsel: "Seek out a place apart, and love the solitary life. Do not engage in conversation with men."[41] The ahistorical, otherworldly character of mysticism is also brought out by the Hindu sage Radhakrishnan: "Religion . . . is essentially the private achievement of the individual won by hard effort in solitude and isolation, on mountain-tops and in monasteries."[42] Emil Brunner observes that the program of mysticism is to find the way to "complete unification with the divine being by plunging into the depth of the soul and by disentangling the soul from all impressions of the outward world."[43]

Such an attitude has profound consequences for the life of worship and prayer. While mystical worship begins by acknowledging the presence, evangelical or prophetic worship begins with an invocation. The highest act of worship for the evangelical Christian is not a mystical flight into solitude but a fellowship meal, a Holy Communion (William Temple).

## DIVERGENT VIEWS ON PRAYER

Given the contrasting attitudes toward God, man and the world, it is not surprising that two palpably different views of prayer can be detected in the spiritualities in question.

Mystical prayer embraces the stages of meditation, contemplation, and ecstasy. First one focuses attention on the being of God (meditation), and then one is taken into or grasped by this being (contemplation). The root meaning of *meditation* is thinking, whereas *contemplation* means seeing. Some scholars of mysticism distinguish between ascetical and mystical prayer: in the former one uses one's own efforts to pray, and in the latter one is pervaded by the spirit of prayer or more correctly by the Spirit of God. Some mystics refer to a transforming union with God in which ecstasies become rare and one experiences complete control of one's body by God. In Quietist mysticism, the ideal is a "holy indifference" which transcends all feelings and raptures.[44]

The mystics see prayer more in terms of the vision of God than of seeking the help of God. Augustine understands prayer as "a loving gaze of the spirit directed towards God."[45] According to Thomas Aquinas, the desire for contemplation arises from the love of the object contemplated because we long to gaze at the object we love.[46] In Tersteegen's view, "Prayer is looking at God, who is ever present, and letting Him look on us."[47] For Thomas Merton, mystical prayer is "wordless and total surrender of the heart in silence."[48]

In theological history, mystical prayer is commonly spoken of as the lifting up of the soul to God. John of Damascus defines prayer as the elevation of the mind and heart to God. Thomas Aquinas refers to "the ascent of the mind to God." True prayer is said to consist in submission and resignation. Confession is not regarded as necessary in pure mysticism, for it is through contemplation that wrongs are dispelled or dissolved. For the anonymous author of *The Cloud of Unknowing*, "prayer is simply a reverent, conscious openness to God full of the desire to grow in goodness and overcome evil."[49] It is not so much a prayer *to* God as a prayer *in* God.

In the monasteries and religious orders that developed in Roman Catholicism and Eastern Orthodoxy, liturgical prayer was also valued highly, and it would seem that this kind of prayer stands in tension with mystical prayer. Yet in many of these circles liturgical prayer is regarded as only a means to the deeper prayer, wordless union with God. According to Thomas Merton, in the tradition of St. Benedict and John Cassian "wordless contemplative prayer in purity of heart, without images or words, even beyond thoughts, could be expected to flower from the active prayer of the liturgy as its normal fulfillment."[50]

Both Christian and non-Christian mystics are in agreement that the highest prayer excludes petition. In mysticism prayer is practicing the presence rather than fervent supplication. Augustine regarded prayer for material goods as "carnal prayer"; to the spiritually twice-born only "spiritual prayer" is seemly. Meister Eckhart declared, "People often say to me: 'Pray for me!' At that I have to wonder . . . why not be your true self and reach into your own treasure? For the whole truth is just as much in you as in me!"[51] When asked, "What is the prayer of the disinterested heart?" he answered, "A disinterested man, pure in heart, has no prayer, for to pray is to want something from God ... he prays only to be uniform with God."[52] The motto of Francis de Sales was "Require nothing, refuse nothing." For Thomas Merton, prayer is not essentially seeking communion but rather realized communion in which we affirm what God gives. According to Aldous Huxley, "the practical teaching of Indian and Christian mystics is identical in such matters as ... renunciation of petitionary prayer in favour of simple abandonment to the will of God."[53] George Maloney grants that while "the simple believers" will continue to appeal to God for aid, the masters of the spiritual life go beyond petition to contemplation where one is emptied of self and taken up into God.[54]

How utterly different is prophetic or evangelical prayer, the pouring out of the heart to God, making known to God one's needs and desires, and beseeching him for aid (cf. 1 Sam. 1:15; Pss. 42:4; 62:8; Matt. 7:7, 8; Phil. 4:6). It is true that the metaphor "lifting up of the soul" or something similar is found in several of the Psalms, but the context plainly indicates that the meaning is bringing before God our innermost needs, not seeking to be lost in the contemplation of God (cf. Pss. 25:1, 2; 86:4–7). In Psalm 123 it is written, "To thee I lift up my eyes," but the psalmist goes on to say, "As the eyes of slaves look to the hand of their master ... so our eyes look to the Lord our God, till he shows us his mercy" (Ps. 123:1, 2, NIV). The object of prayer is not to escape into heaven but to knock on the door of heaven so that our needs can be met in the here and now. (Ps. 4:6; 2 Chron. 32:20; 1 Kings 8:30; Matt. 7:7, 8; Luke 11:9, 10). In Psalm 24:7–10 we are called to lift up the gates of our hearts so that the king of glory might come in; nothing is said here of our being elevated into glory. Prayer in the Psalms is not an ascent to the Godhead but a plea that, it is hoped, will reach the Godhead (cf. Ps. 86:1–4). It is a plea, moreover, that is made possible by the descent of the living God into our midst (cf. Pss. 86:12, 13; 97:11, 12 [NIV]; 98:1, 2; 118:27).

Luther and Calvin both understood prayer as the petitioning of an earnest soul, though they included adoration, thanksgiving and confession within this general orientation. Luther believed that when Christians are in dire straits or despair "there is no other comfort or counsel except in holding fast by prayer and crying to God for help."[55] For Calvin, the best spur to calling upon God is when saints are "distressed by their own need" and "troubled by the greatest unrest."[56] Heiler observes that Luther's piety manifests a distinctly mystical element especially in his earlier years, but it basically mirrors the prophetic thrust of the Bible.[57]

In Puritan spirituality, prayer was seen as "an agonized rending of the garments of the soul." Richard Sibbes defined prayer as "a cry to God with strong supplications."[58] In contrast to the general tenor of mysticism, Sibbes urged us "to bind God" with his own promises and beseech him to do unto us "according to his good word." In this view, prayer sometimes entails contending and battling with God so that we can overcome in and through God.[59] His Christocentric orientation is evident in his contention that "there is no coming to God, no intercourse between God and us immediately, but between [the] God-man and God and us, who is the mediator between God and us."[60] God is no passive Subject on whom we can only gaze in reverent adoration but an Active Agent who is ever at work in and through the faith and prayers of his people: "As faith sets prayer on work, so prayer sets God on work; and when God is set on work by prayer . . . he sets all on work."[61]

Among the radical Pietists mystical themes again came to the fore, but the Reformation element resurfaced in such persons as Jacob Boehme. Although he emphasized detachment from the earthly and the material and stressed the insufficiency of external prayer as opposed to true inward prayer, he meant by the latter the sincere and fervent beseeching of a merciful God. With remarkable similarity to his spiritual forefather Martin Luther, he could give voice to this kind of utterance: "I cry to You in my soul's hunger and pray to You with all my powers."[62] Moreover, like Luther as well as Arndt, he saw the mystical union commencing with the gift of faith in Jesus Christ.

Similarly, Søren Kierkegaard, in whom both mystical and

prophetic motifs can be detected, understood prayer primarily as heartfelt supplication to a holy God.[63] As he graphically described it, "He lets me weep before him in silent solitude, pour forth . . . my pain, with the blessed consolation of knowing that he is concerned for me."[64]

Dietrich Bonhoeffer, whose theological mentors were Luther and Karl Barth, gave poignant expression to the prophetic kind of prayer:

> O God, early in the morning I cry to you.
>   Help me to pray
> And to concentrate my thoughts on you;
>   I cannot do this alone.[65]

Biblical piety insists that our very prayers need to be redeemed, because the person who prays is always a sinner and therefore will invariably allow base and uncharitable motivations to intrude into the life of prayer. According to Calvin, "whenever believers prepare themselves to pray to God, they ought . . . to feel that their prayers are sprinkled by the blood of our Lord Jesus Christ, in order to be pure and clean, and to be received by God as a sweet-smelling sacrifice."[66] Mystics, on the other hand, seek a purer and higher kind of prayer than that which characterizes ordinary mortals, one that transcends the impulses and passions of the flesh, and this higher prayer is a sign that redemption has already been effected in their lives. For biblical, prophetic piety the proper attitude in prayer is a sense of our own unworthiness and helplessness, not an awareness of our natural kinship with God or a burning desire for union with divinity. Daniel Jenkins puts it very succinctly: "The one quality Christian prayer in faith demands from us is not moral excellence nor a spiritual gift nor natural piety but humility, humility to acknowledge our unworthiness of God and our need."[67] And in the judgment of Richard Sibbes, "No man may come to God, but upon his knees. I speak not of the bowing of the knee, but of the heart."[68]

In evangelical spirituality it is acknowledged that though the heart of prayer is supplication, it may also take the form of thanksgiving, confession, and even complaint and question. The stress is on vocal prayer, although it is not denied that there may very well be a place for meditation as a preparation for true prayer. This particular note is not always discernible, however, in the mainstream of evangelical piety. Abraham Kuyper averred that "prayer without words rarely satisfies the soul. Mere mental prayer is necessarily imperfect; earnest, fervent prayer constrains us to express it in words."[69]

Prophetic religion affirms that true prayer not only includes a pleading with God but also a striving or wrestling with God, an effort to change or alter his will. Here we see the struggle and even the presumption in biblical prayer which is conspicuously absent from mystical prayer. David Brainerd, missionary to the American Indians, prayed in the snow until his body was wet with sweat. John Hyde, Presbyterian missionary to India, prayed, "Father, give me these souls, or I die." The believer in prayer is "like a woman with child, who writhes and cries out in her pangs" (Isa. 26:17). Prayer in the biblical sense may sometimes be humiliating and exhausting. According to Adolphe Monod, the mature Christian does not simply ask and hope: he "craves and waits until he has obtained." He does not merely seek God, he "strives with God and triumphs."[70] Sibbes, Moody, Spurgeon, Finney, and many other evangelicals spoke of the power of "prevailing prayer" in which the warrior of faith prevails over what seems to be God's permissive will so that his ultimate will may be brought closer to fulfillment. George Müller of the Plymouth Brethren made a place for "holy argument" in prayer in which we plead our case before the throne of grace.[71] Richard Sibbes also advocated "strong arguments" in prayer, for "they are of use and force to prevail with God."[72]

Forsyth remarked that the ways of God are flexible, though his final will is irrevocable. God makes himself dependent on the pleadings of his children so that his purposes may be realized at least in partial cooperation with his children. Such a view in no way detracts from the sovereignty of God but instead bears witness to its breadth and scope.

Wrestling and pleading with God are regarded with disfavor in the circles of mysticism. Francis de Sales advised: "Guard against all intellectual exertion, for this is harmful in prayer."[73] For Angelus Silesius, "It is meaningless to say 'Thy will be done,' and yet to pray 'Please take this agony away.'"[74] It is our will, not God's will that needs to be changed; therefore it is not for us to entreat God in prayer but instead to submit passively to the divine will. Importunate prayer is foreign to mysticism.

In prophetic prayer one does not passively resign oneself to the will of God; rather, one actively seeks to discover God's will in heartfelt supplication. There is a time for submission, but this is viewed as an active surrender rather than a passive compliance. The Christian places himself at God's disposal and asks how he can best fulfill the divine imperative. We see in evangelical prayer a subordination of one's will to God's will, but not the complete renunciation or negation of one's will, as in mysticism.

In evangelical devotion there is pleading even in the act of surrender. This is evident in the witness of Ann Judson, wife of Adoniram Judson, American Baptist missionary to Burma. She describes her encounter with God when her husband was imprisoned and she was completely immobilized by jungle fever:

> If I ever felt the value and efficacy of prayer, I did at this time. I could not rise from my couch. I could make no efforts to secure my husband. I could only plead with that great and powerful Being who has said, "Call upon me in the day of trouble and I will hear, and thou shalt glorify me." God made me at this time feel so powerfully this promise, that I became quite composed, feeling assured that my prayers would be answered.[75]

Prayer in evangelical perspective is a great socializer. We do not detach ourselves from our fellow human beings but identify ourselves with their sufferings and trials. Intercessory prayer was particularly valued by the Reformers and the evangelical renewal movements subsequent to the Reformation. British Evangelical G. Campbell Morgan declared, "Men only pray with prevailing power who do so amid the sobs and sighing of the race." Group prayer was also held in high regard, in accordance with Jesus' words: "For where two or three are gathered in my name, there am I in the midst of them" (Matt. 18:20).

The note of intercession and supplication is not absent in the Eastern Orthodox and Roman Catholic traditions, and it can be seen particularly in the monastic liturgies. St. Basil defined prayer as a petition or request for some good poured out by the faithful before God.[76] John of Damascus included in prayer "the request for fitting things from God."[77] The Russian Orthodox saint Tikhon of Zadonsk explained:

> As many turn to a good and generous man because they hope to obtain from him what they need, so those who have a firm, untroubled trust in God, rich in charity and generosity, beg from him pardon and assistance. Prayer is a request for something good, addressed to God by pious men.[78]

Christian mysticism is by no means bereft of biblical insights, but its Platonic and Neo-Platonic cast has given it a spiritual orientation quite different from that of biblical, prophetic faith. The aim in mysticism is to ascend from the material to the spiritual, from the visible to the invisible. It seeks to move beyond petitionary prayer and even beyond meditation into contemplative adoration of the being of God. Its goal is to get beyond thought to the experience of Oneness. As Evagrius phrased it, "You will not be able to pray purely if you are . . . involved with material affairs and agitated with unremitting concerns. For prayer is the rejection of concepts."[79]

While mystical spirituality suggests specific techniques for preparing oneself for the higher levels of prayer, prophetic prayer is characterized by freedom and spontaneity.[80] The emphasis of the prophets is not on methods for spiritual nurture but on the divine intrusion into human life that comes unexpectedly and suddenly. In contrast to ritual prayer and the kind of mysticism that encourages the repetitive invocation of the name of Jesus or similar methods in meditation, prophetic spirituality condemns mechanical repetitions in prayer. It should be recognized, however, that the mystics have generally held that the highest stage of prayer, contemplative union, cannot be induced or acquired by spiritual technique but comes to us only as a gift of grace.

In the Christian mystical tradition, as has already been indicated, the historical Christ is only a means to the ahistorical Godhead, the depth and ground of the self and the whole of existence. "In coming to know God in visible form," said Augustine, "we may, through him, be borne up to the love of what is invisible."[81] As Eckhart put it, "We must invoke this 'tent' of the humanity of our Lord Jesus Christ only for the sake of union with the Godhead."[82] For John of the Cross, meditation is "a discursive mental activity by means of images, forms and figures that are produced imaginatively . . . as happens, for example, when we picture in our imagination Christ crucified."[83] But he went on to say, "The soul must be emptied of all these imagined forms, figures, and images, and it must remain in darkness in respect to these internal senses if it is to attain Divine union."

The mystics following Plotinus have commonly referred to the need for simplification, the divesting oneself of external images, the abandonment of words and concepts. For Louis Merton, "the highest form of prayer is . . . a prayer 'without forms,' a pure prayer in which there are no longer any images or ideas, and in which the spirit does not take any initiative of its own, for all activity of the human mind and senses is here completely surpassed."[84] Teresa of Avila described the state of contemplation as "a sleep of the faculties."[85] In Eastern Orthodox mysticism, even the name of Jesus may finally have to be set aside as the soul prepares for union with the Eternal:

> The Name is only an incentive to and support to the Presence. A time may come, even here on earth, when we have to discard the Name itself and to become free from everything but the nameless and unutterable living contact with the Person of Jesus.[86]

In pure mysticism the goal is a detachment from feelings. Fénelon could speak of a "love without feelings." According to Eckhart, we must give up even our attachment to peace and quiet in the "breakthrough to the Godhead." Evangelical spirituality, by contrast, seeks a redirection of but not a negation or suppression of our feelings.

Moreover, for the mystics God speaks to us primarily through solitude and silence rather than through his Word understood as the verbal proclamation of the evangel. The hallmark of mysticism is a direct experience of God. Even the Reformed mystic Tersteegen, who manifested a deep biblical faith, declared that God can and does work without any external medium.

While prophetic prayer is social, mystical religion is individualistic and nonsocial. The goal of prophetic prayer is the realization of all ethical and spiritual values, the coming of the dynamic kingdom of God. Mystical prayer aspires to the ultimate supreme good, a static final good, or to a reality beyond good and evil.

## POSSIBILITY OF CONVERGENCE?

Can there be a convergence between these two types of spirituality? There can certainly be no synthesis where mysticism emerges as the higher or purer type. Yet some of the criticisms of mysticism, especially those of Brunner and Kraemer, may be too harsh. Does mysticism mirror only the sinful craving for divinity, as Kraemer suggests, or does it not also reflect our deepest yearnings for a true experience of God? Is there not a mystical element in biblical religion itself which should perhaps be explored?

German Protestant theology has often made a distinction between *Mystik*, referring to a type of experience, and *Mystizismus*, denoting a type of piety or religion or philosophy. Biblical faith stands in diametrical opposition to mysticism as "the perennial philosophy," as Aldous Huxley has described it, but it does not necessarily deny the validity of the mystical experience, the experience of self-transcendence in which we are grasped by the divine presence.

Although mystical awareness is not yet faith, we must ask whether faith itself contains a mystical element. Is not faith a self-transcending experience as well as trust and obedience? Are not feeling and ecstasy included in the act of faith as well as knowledge? Does not faith involve an identification with the sufferings of Christ, an inward spiritual union with Christ?

In examining the spirituality of Martin Luther, one can detect a persistent mystical element which extends even to his later writings. For Luther, *ecstasis* (ecstasy), so popular among medieval mystics, was associated with *fides*, which occurs at the beginning, not the end of the Christian pilgrimage. The mystical term *excessus* (transfiguration) was also occasionally employed to describe faith. Moreover, Luther made a sharp distinction between "historical faith" and "true faith," which involves "immediate," "direct" feeling.

Admittedly Christian prayer is directed to the Father in heaven, but its ground is the indwelling Spirit. We must also ask whether there is not an inseparable relation between supplication and meditation and whether the former does not presuppose the latter. Can we pray to a God on whose mighty acts we never or seldom reflect? The prayers in Old Testament history frequently grew out of and included a recollection of the acts of deliverance that God had wrought for his people.[87] Luther stressed the need for meditation on the passion of Christ but with the express purpose of reminding us of our sin and constraining us to pray for forgiveness. Cannot we even speak of union with God as one of the goals of prayer, if we here mean union with his will as revealed in Christ, not absorption into his being, as mystics of the monistic stripe envision this?

On the Catholic side, Hans Urs von Balthasar has sought to correct the imbalances in devotional life brought about by an all too ready acceptance of mystical or Platonic ideas: "Contemplative prayer ... neither can nor should be self-contemplation, but a reverent regard and listening to what is characterized in

its inmost being as the Not-me, namely the word of God."[88]
Moreover, "it is a mistake," he contends, "to regard *oratio* as inferior to *contemplatio*, and to view vocal prayer as primarily for beginners and contemplative prayer as suitable mainly for the advanced. Each depends on the other and presupposes it, and the one should lead directly into the other."[89]

In a similar manner, the Dominican scholar Simon Tugwell confesses that "our spirituality has for a very long time been heavily conditioned by a mystical theology centred on God's eternal being, in one form or another. Some writers have even encouraged us to leave behind all consideration of the Incarnate Christ, let alone prayer of petition."[90] He goes on to point out that the "prayer of petition, and especially intercession, is a prophetic function, to be exercised . . . by those endowed with the divine Spirit."[91]

My thesis is that there is a necessary place for meditation and contemplative adoration in evangelical piety, though these should never be regarded as surrogates for prayer. Surely there is a need to direct our attention to heavenly or spiritual themes. St. Paul calls us to fix our thoughts on things above (Col. 3:2; Phil. 4:8). The psalmist declares, "On the glorious splendor of thy majesty, and on thy wondrous works, I will meditate" (Ps. 145:5). And again: "I will meditate on thy precepts, and fix my eyes on thy ways. I will delight in thy statutes; I will not forget thy word" (Ps. 119:15, 16). In the Bible degrading, fearful thoughts are seen as an abomination to God (cf. Deut. 20:8; Prov. 15:26; 18:20, 21; Matt. 6:25 ff.). Sibbes regarded it as "Christian wisdom, to fix our souls on good meditations, to have them wedded to good thoughts," for such cogitations "may lead us comfortably in our way to heaven."[92] This biblical view is also reflected in Bonhoeffer: "Above all, we should avoid getting absorbed in the present moment, and foster that peace of mind which springs from noble thoughts, measuring all other things by them."[93] In the Old Testament, we are urged to meditate on the law of God; New Testament faith encourages us to meditate on Jesus Christ, the One who embodies and fulfills the law.

Meditation in the evangelical sense is always grounded in and gives rise to supplication. We seek to meditate on divine things out of a need to draw closer to God and receive the assurance of his pardon and favor. We should pray that the Spirit of God might guide us in our meditation even as we prepare to enter into dialogue with God during and following our meditation.

Our goal in this kind of spiritual exercise is not simply *detachment* from the world but a richer *attachment* to God and to other human beings. As people united with Christ, we seek power and boldness for service in his kingdom. Calvin contended that through meditation on things divine we "may refresh our languishing spirits with new vigor."[94]

The focus in evangelical meditation is not on the experience of inwardness (as in much popular mysticism) but on the biblical story of reconciliation and redemption in Jesus Christ. Our thoughts should be directed not even to the Godhead as such but to the Word made flesh, God incarnate. Von Balthasar is emphatic that we should not try to contemplate God's life in the Trinity itself but only his life in the incarnation of his Son, for it is in Jesus Christ alone that we know God.[95]

That evangelical tradition has given a prominent role to meditation is attested in its hymns and gospel songs, which take the form not only of supplication and intercession but also of praise and adoration, as well as reflection on the goodness of creation and the mystery of salvation. This reflection is geared, however, not to a transcendence of the temporal and material but to their transfiguration by the grace of regeneration.

John Owen, the Puritan divine, recommended frequent meditation on "the holy excellencies of the divine nature" as well as on the mediation and intercession of Jesus as "a most useful preparation for prayer."[96] Such a practice will promote our likeness to Christ, for "our minds will be changed into the image of what we contemplate."[97]

In Theodore G. Brakel, a Dutch Pietist in the early seventeenth century, we see at least a partial synthesis of mystical and ethical elements. While he stressed the following of Christ in the midst of our ordinary duties in life, he spent much time in solitary prayer and meditation. This was the result:

> Praying in that particular way and reminding God of his promises I was finally transported into such a state of joy and my thoughts were so drawn upward that, seeing God with the eyes of my soul, I felt one with him. I felt myself transported into God's being and at the same time I was so filled with joy, peace, and sweetness, that I cannot express it. With my spirit I was entirely in heaven for two or three days.[98]

Evangelical piety insists that meditation always be related to action. It is intended not to direct us into ourselves, to the ground of our being, but to lead us out of ourselves into the work of the kingdom. Jeremy Taylor advised meditating until one is moved to some act of piety relating to the theme of the meditation. In his *Life Together* Bonhoeffer maintained that meditation not only strengthens faith by fostering a deeper communion with God but also impels one to active service in the world. According to Olive Wyon, meditation should be closed with a short prayer and a practical resolution.

This note can also be discerned among many of the Catholic mystics. Fénelon contended that our meditation should issue in a resolution before God and a petition "to inspire us to accomplish what he gives us the courage to promise him."[99] Francis de Sales recommended closing our meditations in acts of thanksgiving, offering, and supplication. By this he meant that we should offer resolutions united with the offering of Christ and plead that he might grant us the grace to fulfill them.[100]

Contemplation in evangelical spirituality is to be understood not as an intuitive apprehension of the essence of God but simply as loving, heartfelt attention to the things of God. Neither meditation nor contemplation is to be regarded as true prayer. They are at best salutary devotional exercises which both precede and follow prayer. Mystical or mental prayer is not higher than the prayer of faith. I cannot subscribe to the Hindu maxim "Prayer is speaking to God. Meditation is letting God speak to you." We walk by faith alone, not by a mystical apprehension or direct vision of God.

Meditation, like prayer, has as its aim the glorification of God. In the words of the psalmist: "May my meditation be pleasing to him, for I rejoice in the Lord" (Ps. 104:34). We use silence not to get beyond the Word (as in mysticism) but to prepare ourselves to hear the Word. It is also conducive to reflection upon the Word.

Petitionary prayer remains primary because throughout life the Christian is completely dependent on God. Wesley maintained that even in the state of Christian perfection the sanctified Christian still needs Christ as Prophet, Priest, and King. Even in the so-called realm of Paradise, the intermediate state between death and the final resurrection, the saints are busily engaged in intercessory prayer on behalf of the church militant.

There is, of course, an undeniable place for adoration and thanksgiving in biblical piety. Yet our purpose in giving praise to God is not to extricate ourselves from earthly cares and responsibilities but to demonstrate our gratefulness for God's gift of Jesus Christ. We are also moved to thank God for the wonder of his created world, not for the privilege of rising above the world.

In the circles of radical mysticism, which include the Quietists, Madame Guyon and Molinos, even the prayers of thanksgiving and praise are rejected. Just as one is not permitted to ask God for anything, so one may not thank him for anything, since both are acts of one's own will.

Evangelical, prophetic prayer is prayer from the heart. It does not consist in vain repetitions and magical incantations as in primitive and ritual prayer. Nor is it a technique that focuses attention exclusively on God or Jesus. Ideally, it is free prayer, not read or recited prayer. The prayer of the heart bursts through all external aids and formulas that might be employed to deepen devotion.

This is not to deny the rightful place for aids in the life of prayer and devotion. In order to help the earnest Christian, Luther suggested that morning and evening devotions be opened with the sign of the cross and include the Lord's Prayer and Apostles' Creed as well as the singing of a hymn. The reading of Psalms before or after prayer has also been recommended by spiritual writers in the evangelical as well as the mystical traditions. In the judgment of Richard Sibbes: *"The nearer we are to God, the more in love we will be with spiritual exercises;* the more near to God, the more in love with all means to draw nigh to him."[101] Yet evangelical religion insists that the people of God not become bound to any ritual or formula, nor should they pin their faith and hope on these things, which should be seen as crutches for believers as they struggle toward a more perfect faith. At the same time, all Christians are on the way to perfection; none of us has arrived at the place where we can dispense with the means of grace, and I here include not only Scripture reading and hymns but also the hearing of the preached Word and the sacraments. It is mysticism, not evangelical religion, that seeks finally to transcend the means of grace.

In biblical spirituality, there is a need for common prayer as well as solitary devotions. The evangelical ideal is not the "flight of the alone to the alone" (Plotinus) but fellowship with God and all the saints. The psalmist declared, "I will give thanks to the Lord with my whole heart, in the company of the upright, in the congregation" (Ps. 111:1). True prayer, however personal and solitary, is never exclusively private. One can be in physical solitude, but one is never spiritually alone. Cardinal Newman confessed, "I am never less alone than when I am all alone."

Jesus is, of course, our model, especially in the spiritual life. He prayed in the synagogue and in the wilderness, and though he withdrew at times from his disciples, he never remained apart. He wrestled with God and interceded for humankind. He poured out his heart before God, as did the great prophets in Israelite history (Heb. 5:7). He was also united with God in daily, constant communion. He offered his petitions to his heavenly Father but at the same time subordinated his will to the will of his Father.

Despite a marked openness to mysticism Nathan Söderblom, renowned ecumenical Lutheran theologian, contends that the prayer life of Jesus was radically different from the ideal of classical mysticism.

> So much we may know with absolute certainty from all the Gospel tells of Jesus, that his prayer never was merely a state of soul attained by some sure method, an *oratio mentalis,* a Prayer of Quiet, a meditation, but an intercourse and conversation with the heavenly Father, an outlet for anguish and uncertainty and for questions that needed answer; the bursting forth of a tone of jubilation, a trembling yet confident intimacy longing for undisturbed intercourse with the Father in Heaven, although the feeling of nearness and fellowship with him was wont never to cease during the duties and occupations of the day.[102]

Friedrich Heiler perceptively observes that mystical prayer has a marked sublimity, because it is free from the egoism, eudaemonism, and anthropomorphism of primitive prayer. He acknowledges that even prophetic prayer "does not show that refinement, tenderness, and world-denying spirituality" characteristic of mystical prayer. Nor does it manifest "the impressive movement of mystical prayer." Nonetheless, he contends that "the prayer of the Bible and the Reformation in its unpretentious simplicity and childlike sincerity of heart, in its healthy passion and original, native power stands incomparably nearer to genuinely human feelings than contemplative, mystical devotion in its calm renunciation and majestic solemnity, its melting tenderness and consuming, passionate surrender."[103] These are precisely my own sentiments.

## NOTES

1. Hoffman suggests that Luther remained indebted to the mystics for many of his basic insights. See Bengt R. Hoffman, *Luther and the Mystics* (Minneapolis: Augsburg, 1976). Steven Ozment convincingly argues, however, that the originality of Luther has been lost in the attempt to forge an ecu-

menical breakthrough. See Steven E. Ozment, *Homo Spiritualis* (Leiden: Brill, 1969). For my appraisal of both these scholars see *supra*, pp. 2, 3.

2. In other noted mystics in the modern age, such as Joel Goldsmith, Kahlil Gibran, Krishnamurti, and Aldous Huxley, Christian motifs are only dimly reflected, if at all. In Thomas Merton Neo-Platonic and biblical motifs exist side by side, but the former predominate.

3. The etymological roots of "mysticism" are to be traced to the Greek words *mystikos*, which means hidden or secret, and *mueō*, which means to shut one's eyes or mouth. The earliest use of *mystikos* in pre-Christian times is in connection with the mystery religions, whose essential rites were kept hidden except from the initiated. It later came to signify an immediate awareness or direct experience of the divine presence, an experience that bypasses the senses.

4. See *supra*, pp. 3 ff.

5. Friedrich Heiler, *Prayer*, trans. and ed. Samuel McComb (New York: Oxford University Press, 1958), p. 170.

6. Emil Brunner, *Truth as Encounter*, trans. Amandus W. Loos and David Cairns (Philadelphia: Westminster Press, 1964), p. 90. For Brunner's critique of the mysticism of Schleiermacher, see Emil Brunner, *Die Mystik und das Wort* (Tübingen: Mohr, 1928).

7. Hendrik Kraemer, *Religion and the Christian Faith* (London: Lutterworth Press, 1956), p. 335.

8. Baron Friedrich von Hügel, *The Life of Prayer* (London: Dent, 1960), p. 43.

9. Hans Küng, *Freedom Today*, trans. Cecily Hastings (New York: Sheed & Ward, 1966), pp. 136, 137.

10. R. C. Zaehner, *Zen, Drugs and Mysticism* (New York: Pantheon, 1972), p. 78.

11. See Thomas Molnar, *God and the Knowledge of Reality* (New York: Basic Books, 1973).

12. Matthew Fox, "Spirituality for Protestants," *The Christian Century*, 95, no. 25, (1978): 731–736. Fox's position is not the same as that of the Reformation, which emphasizes redemption through the vicarious substitutionary atonement of Christ on the cross and sees creation in the service of this redemption. Fox's spirituality resembles more a process-oriented or worldly mysticism. He appears to reject not only Neo-Platonism but also biblical theism in his preference for a naturalistic panentheism.

13. John of Ruysbroeck, *The Adornment of the Spiritual Marriage, Etc.*, Bk. 2, Ch. 65, ed. Evelyn Underhill, trans. C. A. Wynschenk Dom (London: Dent, 1916), p. 150.

14. *Meister Eckhart*, ed. and trans. Raymond B. Blakney (New York: Harper, 1941), p. 100.

15. John Calvin, *Sermons on the Epistle to the Ephesians* (Edinburgh: Banner of Truth Trust, 1975), p. 19.

16. Martin Luther, *The Table Talk of Martin Luther*, ed. Thomas Kepler (Cleveland: World, 1952), p. 143.

17. Dom Cuthbert Butler, *Western Mysticism* (New York: Barnes & Noble, 1968), pp. xxvii, xxviii. The quotation is from Dom Augustine Baker.

18. Thomas Merton, *The Ascent to Truth* (New York: Harcourt, Brace, 1951), p. 83.

19. Wm. Johnston, ed., *The Cloud of Unknowing and the Book of Privy Counseling* (Garden City, N.Y.: Doubleday, 1973), p. 149.

20. Reinhold Niebuhr, *Christian Realism and Political Problems* (New York: Scribner's, 1953), pp. 139, 140.

21. Anders Nygren, *Agape and Eros,* trans. Philip S. Watson, rev. ed. (Philadelphia: Westminster Press, 1953).

22. Albrecht Ritschl, *Three Essays,* trans. and ed. Philip Hefner (Philadelphia: Fortress Press, 1972), p. 76.

23. Catherine of Siena, *The Dialogue of the Seraphic Virgin,* chap. 64.

24. The tension between prophetic and mystical religion is much more pronounced when the comparison is with Buddhist rather than Christian mysticism. See Isidor Thorner, "Prophetic and Mystic Experience," *Journal for the Scientific Study of Religion,* 5, no. 1 (1965): 82–96.

25. An evangelical as well as a Neo-Platonic strand are conspicuous in Augustine, Anselm, Thomas Aquinas, Bonaventura, Bernard of Clairvaux, and Gerhard Tersteegen. Heiler convincingly maintains that evangelical motifs are subordinated to Neo-Platonic mysticism even in these persons, though some scholars would dispute this. Mystics in whom Neo-Platonism (or some kindred form of mysticism) is much more dominant include Dionysius the pseudo-Areopagite, Evagrius Ponticus, John Scotus Erigena, Meister Eckhart, John Tauler, Catherine of Genoa, and Angelus Silesius. Rudolf Otto argues with some cogency that the mysticism of Eckhart is qualitatively different from that of Dionysius and Plotinus because of his emphasis on ethical action in the world. (See Rudolf Otto, *Mysticism East and West* [New York: Meridian Books, 1957]). My position is that biblical motifs are definitely present in Eckhart but that they are obscured by a Neo-Platonic cast.

26. S. Radhakrishnan, *The Hindu View of Life* (London: Allen & Unwin, 1961), p. 23.

27. Quoted in Evelyn Underhill, *The Mystics of the Church* (New York: Schocken, 1964), p. 165.

28. Thomas Merton, *Thoughts in Solitude* (New York: Farrar, Straus & Cudahy, 1958), p. 17.

29. It is well to note that the ideology of feminism promotes the mystical as opposed to the prophetic understanding of God. In ideological feminism, God is no longer the Father Almighty who created heaven and earth but the eternal ground of being or the regenerative process within nature. See Mary Daly, *Beyond God the Father* (Boston: Beacon Press, 1973). C. S. Lewis holds that the conflict between prophetic and mystical religion has its roots in the tension between the primeval myths of the Sky Father and the Earth Mother.

30. Note that Exodus 3:14 can be translated "I will be who I will be." Even the

translation "I am that I am" connotes being in action, not motionless, static being.

31. Quoted in Johnston, *The Cloud of Unknowing*, p. 187.
32. Karl Rahner, *Theological Investigations*, Vol. 5, trans. Karl-H. Kruger (Baltimore: Helicon Press, 1966), p. 97.
33. Butler, *Western Mysticism*, p. 117.
34. Thomas Merton calls Bernard of Clairvaux a "mystic of light" and John of the Cross a "mystic of night," although even the latter speaks of the love and joy that overwhelm the creature in the state of contemplative union with God. In Merton, *The Ascent to Truth*, pp. 217 ff.
35. See the discussion in Butler, *Western Mysticism*, pp. lxix ff.
36. John Telford, ed., *The Letters of the Rev. John Wesley* (London: Epworth Press, 1931), Vol. 6, p. 272.
37. In Heiler, *Prayer*, p. 139.
38. Thomas Aquinas, *Summa Contra Gentiles*, bk. 3, chap. 117.
39. Bernard of Clairvaux, Sermon 40, *Sermones in Cantica Canticorum*, in J.-P. Migne, ed., *Patrologia Latina* (Paris, 1854), 183: 983.
40. Walter Hilton, *The Scale of Perfection*, trans. Leo Sherley-Price, new abridged ed. (St. Meinrad, Ind.: Abbey Press, 1975), p. 41.
41. Thomas à Kempis, *The Imitation of Christ*, trans. Leo Sherley-Price (Baltimore: Penguin, 1959), p. 164.
42. S. Radhakrishnan, *East and West in Religion* (London: Allen & Unwin, 1967), p. 54. Cf.: "The Eastern religions are directed to the salvation of the individual soul rather than to the maintenance of society" (p. 56).
43. Emil Brunner, *The Scandal of Christianity* (Philadelphia: Westminster Press, 1951), p. 19.
44. This "holy indifference" of Quietism bears a remarkable similarity to the Buddha's "way of selflessness" and the self-forgetfulness of Taoism.
45. In Jean Daujat, *Prayer* (New York: Hawthorne Books, 1964), p. 46.
46. Thomas Aquinas, *Scriptum super libros Sententiarum*, Vol. 3, dis. 27.
47. Gerhard Tersteegen, *The Quiet Way* (New York: Philosophical Library, 1950), p. 23.
48. Thomas Merton, *Contemplative Prayer* (Garden City, N.Y.: Doubleday/Image Books, 1971), p. 30.
49. Johnston, *The Cloud of Unknowing*, p. 98.
50. Merton, *Contemplative Prayer*, p. 47.
51. Eckhart, *Meister Eckhart*, p. 128.
52. *Ibid.*, pp. 88, 89.
53. Christopher Isherwood, ed., *Vedanta for the Western World* (New York: Viking Press, 1945), p. 105.
54. See Arthur N. Winter, "Exploring Prayer with Father George Maloney," *National Catholic Reporter*, 15, no. 3 (1978): 9–16.
55. In Heiler, *Prayer*, p. 231.
56. Calvin, *Institutes*, III, 20, 11. ed. McNeill, p. 863.
57. Luther's break with mysticism is apparent when he says: "'To come to the Father' is not as with the mystics "to ascend as on wings to heaven, but

with heartfelt confidence to commit oneself to Him as to a gracious Father." Heiler, *Prayer*, p. 156. Cf.: "Do not seek the Spirit through solitude or through prayer, but read Scripture. When a man feels that what he is reading is pleasing to him, let him give thanks; for these are the first fruits of the Spirit." Martin Luther, *Luther's Works*, ed. J. Pelikan., Vol. 29 (St. Louis: Concordia, 1968), p. 83.

58. Cf. "Prayers are cries in affliction. They are not cold dull things, but set on fire: they set the spirit on work to cry to God with earnest, frequent, and fervent prayer." Sibbes, *Complete Works*, Vol. 3, p. 103.

59. Cf.: "He that wrestleth with God shall overcome, and he that overcometh shall have a crown"—Sibbes, *Complete Works*, Vol. 6, p. 307.

60. Sibbes, *Complete Works*, Vol. 4, p. 212.

61. Sibbes, *Complete Works*, Vol. 3, p. 185.

62. *Jacob Boehme—The Way to Christ*, trans. Peter Erb (New York: Paulist, Press, 1978), p. 42. Bornkamm has correctly pointed out that Jacob Boehme can be described as a voluntaristic mystic.

63. In his later years Kierkegaard moved away from the prayer of importunity: "For some time now my praying has been different, actually a calm leaving of everything to God." In *Søren Kierkegaard's Journals and Papers*, Vol. 6, Part 2, ed. and trans. Howard V. Hong and Edna H. Hong (Bloomington: Indiana University Press, 1978), p. 470.

64. Perry D. Le Fevre, ed., *The Prayers of Kierkegaard* (Chicago: University of Chicago Press, 1963), p. 203.

65. Dietrich Bonhoeffer, *Letters and Papers from Prison*, ed. Eberhard Bethge, Enlarged ed. (New York: Macmillan, 1971), p. 139.

66. John Calvin, *The Gospel According to Isaiah*, trans. Leroy Nixon (Grand Rapids, Mich.: Eerdmans, 1953), p. 129.

67. Daniel T. Jenkins, *Prayer and the Service of God* (London: Morehouse-Gorham, 1945), pp. 51, 52.

68. Sibbes, *Complete Works*, Vol. 7, p. 234.

69. Abraham Kuyper, *The Work of the Holy Spirit*, trans. Henri De Vries (Grand Rapids, Mich.: Eerdmans, 1900), p. 623.

70. In Ernest Gordon, *A Book of Protestant Saints* (Three Hills, Alberta: Prairie Bible Institute, 1968), p. 197.

71. See Arthur T. Pierson, *George Müller of Bristol* (Bromley, England: Send the Light Trust, 1975), pp. 146–151. (Reprint.)

72. Sibbes, *Complete Works*, Vol. 6, p. 95. Cf.: "It is good to think of prevailing arguments; not to move God so much as our own hearts; to strengthen our faith to prevail with God, which is much fortified with the consideration of Christ's wondrous loving expression to his poor church"—*Complete Works*, Vol. 2, p. 69.

73. In Walter Nigg, *Great Saints*, trans. William Stirling (Hinsdale, Ill.: Regnery, 1948), p. 200.

74. Angelus Silesius, *The Book of Angelus Silesius*, trans. Frederick Franck (New York: Vintage Books, 1976), p. 117.

75. Cited in Edith Deen, *Great Women of the Christian Faith* (New York: Harper & Row, 1959), p. 177.

76. Aelred Squire, *Asking the Fathers* (New York: Morehouse-Barlow, 1973), p. 200.
77. John of Damascus, *De Fid. Orth.*, 3:24. In Aelred Squire, *Asking the Fathers*, p. 144.
78. Cited in Sergius Bolshakoff, *Russian Mystics* (Kalamazoo, Mich.: Cistercian Publications, 1977), pp. 70, 71. In Tikhon, biblical piety prevails over the Hesychast spirituality of classical Eastern Orthodoxy. References to the fathers and mystics are rare, whereas references to Scripture abound. Yet he also affirmed inward or mental prayer and made a place for contemplation in the Christian life.
79. Cited in John Meyendorff, *St. Gregory Palamas and Orthodox Spirituality*, trans. Adele Fiske (Crestwood, N.Y.: St. Vladimir's Seminary Press, 1974) p. 22. Note that Meyendorff, an Eastern Orthodox theologian, is highly critical of the Neo-Platonism of Evagrius, which affirms "the natural divinity of the human mind" (p. 23).
80. See *Infra*, pp. 122, 123.
81. Quoted in Hans Urs von Balthasar, *Prayer*, trans. A. V. Littledale (New York: Paulist Press, 1961), p. 208.
82. Eckhart, *Meister Eckhart*, p. 200.
83. John of the Cross, *Ascent of Mount Carmel*, BK II, Ch. XII, 3.
84. Louis Merton, "The Humanity of Christ in Monastic Prayer," *Monastic Studies*, no. 2 (1964), p. 7.
85. E. Allison Peers, trans. and ed., *The Complete Works of Saint Teresa of Jesus* (New York: Sheed & Ward, 1946), Vol. 1, p. 96.
86. In *On the Invocation of the Name of Jesus*, by an Eastern Orthodox monk. Trans. Frederick John Nash, Helle Georgiadis, and Joan Ford (London: Fellowship of St. Alban & St. Sergius, 1949), p. 32.
87. See C. W. F. Smith, "Prayer," in *The Interpreter's Dictionary of the Bible*, ed. George A. Buttrick (Nashville, Tenn.: Abingdon Press, 1962), pp. 858–860.
88. Balthasar, *Prayer*, p. 93.
89. *Ibid.*, p. 198.
90. Simon Tugwell, *Did You Receive the Spirit?* (New York: Paulist Press, 1972), p. 60. Note that Tugwell is a leading figure in the Catholic charismatic movement.
91. *Ibid.*
92. Sibbes, *Complete Works*, Vol. 1, p. 329.
93. Dietrich Bonhoeffer, *Letters and Papers from Prison*, ed. Eberhard Bethge (London: SCM Press, 1967), p. 241.
94. Calvin, *Institutes*, ed. McNeill, III, 20, 13, p. 867.
95. Balthasar, *Prayer*, p. 154.
96. John Owen, *The Holy Spirit: His Gifts and Power* (Grand Rapids: Kregel Publications, 1967), p. 336.
97. John Owen, *A Discourse Concerning the Holy Spirit* (Philadelphia: Presbyterian Board of Publication, n.d.), Bk. 5, p. 334.
98. Cited in F. Ernest Stoeffler, *The Rise of Evangelical Pietism* (Leiden: Brill, 1965), p. 149.

99. François Fénelon, *Christian Perfection,* ed. Charles Whiston; trans. Mildred Whitney Stillman (New York: Harper, 1947), p. 70.
100. Francis de Sales, *Introduction to the Devout Life,* trans. and ed. John K. Ryan (London: Longmans, Green, 1953), pp. 65, 66.
101. Sibbes, *Complete Works,* Vol. 7, p. 77.
102. Nathan Söderblom, *The Living God* (Boston: Beacon Press, 1962), p. 59.
103. Heiler, *Prayer,* p. 226.

# VII

# Prayer and Action

## THE LABOR OF PRAYER

Prayer has reference both to God and to the world. It proceeds in two ways—*upward* to God in adoration and supplication, and *outward* to the world in intercession. One might say that prayer is a vertical relation with a horizontal awareness. It concerns active service as well as worship. The soundness of a prayer is measured not by our feelings or fervor at the time but by our behavior afterwards.

Prayer is both a means to action and the highest form of action. Kierkegaard declared, "The best help in all action is to pray; that is true genius; then one never goes wrong."[1] Prayer aids our work in the world, but prayer itself is work—a work of faith. As Forsyth phrased it, "Great worship of God is also a great engagement of ourselves, a great committal of our action."[2] While the mystics often speak of prayer as an end in itself, they redefine it as prayerfulness or communion. Pure mysticism, unlike biblical personalism, does not see the dialectical relationship between prayer and action in the world.[3]

Although it is the highest form of action, prayer is not the only form of Christian action. Deeds of lovingkindness and works of social reform also comprise a necessary part of the Christian life, but they must always be informed by prayer. It can be said that the glory of God is the goal of prayer; social service is the fruit or consequence of prayer.

Forsyth was surely correct in maintaining that "the worst sin is prayerlessness," since this connotes indifference toward God.[4] Just as prayer is the cardinal evidence of faith, so prayerlessness is the salient hallmark of unbelief.

In the circles of mysticism, it is customary to speak of prayer as "holy passivity" and "holy inactivity." Yet prayer is itself a struggle, a work, a discipline. It is not simply waiting on God but taking hold of God (Isa. 64:7). Prayer is "the gymnasium of the soul" (Samuel Zwemer). Tertullian contended that prayer involves "a kind of holy violence to God," because it consists in fervent and unceasing supplication.

The Bible is clear that we must be constant and vigilant in our prayer life, and this entails imposing upon ourselves a prayer discipline. "You will never aspire to pray," said Calvin, "unless you urge and force yourselves."[5] Similarly, for Angela of Foligno the prayer that is most acceptable to God is that which is made by force and constraint. According to Ladislaus Boros, "A special exertion, namely practice in prayer, is necessary in order to become familiar with God, to enjoy having to do with him. It must be worked at, faithfully and with self-discipline; again and again, always anew."[6] And, in the words of an early desert father, "Believe me, I think there is nothing which requires more effort than to pray to God. . . . Prayer demands combat to the last breath."[7] The motif of struggle in prayer is also clearly evident in Luther: "Prayer is indeed a continuous violent action of the spirit as it is lifted up to God. This action is comparable to that of a ship going against the stream."[8]

Prayer, to be sure, is a gift of God. We could not pray unless we were moved by the Holy Spirit to do so. Yet this gift must be appropriated and realized through unceasing and vigilant activity. Prayer is not simply a gift but also a conquest; it is not just an openness to God but a dramatic interaction with God.

Prayer is faith in action. It is a mighty action of the soul, not merely friendly conversation. It involves both a holy passivity and intense activity. It is, in Spurgeon's words, "the shout of the fighting believer." Karl Barth speaks of "the haste and restlessness of the prayer which runs to God and beseeches Him."[9] Prayer is the lever which forces open the iron chest of sacred mystery so that we may obtain the treasure hidden therein (Charles Spurgeon). According to Luther, prayer is "the hardest work of all . . ." "a labour above all labours since he who prays must wage a mighty warfare against the doubt and murmuring excited by the faintheartedness and unworthiness we feel within us."[10]

The best preparation for prayer is prayer itself. When we cannot find words to express our needs to God, we should at least stammer or make the effort. Sibbes observes that just "as every grace increaseth by exercise of itself, so doth the grace of prayer. By prayer we learn to pray."[11] Similarly, Forsyth urges, "To learn to pray with freedom, force yourself to pray."[12] What seems like drudgery can become enjoyment. The Benedictine motto was *Orare est laborare* ("to pray is to work").

Prayer consists in wrestling with God and with ourselves. It also entails battling with the powers of darkness. As Christians, we are called to struggle with the principalities and powers, the spiritual forces of darkness who are superior to humanity though inferior to God (Eph. 6:12). Jesus wrestled with the demonic adversary of God and man in the wilderness (Matt. 4:1–11), and so should we as his followers. Just as he decisively triumphed over the powers of darkness, so may we triumph in and through him.

Our Lord's recommendation is to "first bind the strong man" by the power of faith before we enter his domain and seek to win souls for the kingdom (Matt. 12:29, KJV). The "strong man" here represents the devil, though the devil is himself an agent of the wrath of God, and in fighting the devil we are at the same time trying to stay the severe hand of God's judgment. The demonic forces, to be sure, are diametrically opposed to the revealed will and purpose of God, but they are nonetheless used by God even against their wills, and we can presume often without their knowledge.

Adolphe Monod, Huguenot revivalist of the nineteenth century, graphically describes the struggle of the Christian against the Evil One:

> Blest, when assaulted by the tempter's power,
>   The Cross my armour, and the Lamb my Tower,
> Kneeling I triumph—issuing from the fray
>   A bleeding conqueror—my life a prey.[13]

Mystical religion is accustomed to uphold the prayer of resignation, and indeed there is a time to surrender and submit to God's will. Yet the prayer of resignation can be a testimony of sloth, not faith. True prayer will compel us to resist the desire to resign from the struggle.

Like faith itself, prayer is an unceasing combat with the world, the self, the devil, and even with God. The prayer life entails constant vigilance against distractions and allurements that turn our attention from the things of God.

Prayer is indeed the most difficult task possible for man. As Sibbes tells us, "It is no easy matter to say in truth of heart, *My God;* the flesh will still labour for supremacy."[14] Prayer in the right manner demands full concentration. To devote ourselves to this holy task does not necessarily imply seclusion or renunciation of the good things of life, though sometimes it does mean this. It will always call for concentration, persistence, and perseverance. Andrew Murray considers prayer "the highest part of the work entrusted to us, the root and strength of all other work."[15] True prayer is a hymn more than a cry (Forsyth), a commitment to service rather than renunciation of the world. It is humiliating and sometimes physically exhausting. One should never break off from prayer except in emergencies when the welfare of our neighbor is at stake. The chief failure in prayer is its cessation (Forsyth).

O. Hallesby, whose theology of prayer incorporated a strong

mystical element, nonetheless acknowledged that "the secret prayer chamber is a bloody battleground. Here violent and decisive battles are fought out. Here the fate of souls for time and eternity is determined, in quietude and solitude."[16]

We strive with God not for the purpose of making him kind or generous but rather to gain his attention and make known to him the extremity of our need (cf. Hos. 12:3, 4). Our aim is not to wrest favors from him but to realize his purposes more adequately. He already knows our needs, but he wishes us to come to a full realization of these needs as well before he deigns to act to fulfill them. He wishes us to be earnest in our requests. When God chooses to wait before answering our prayer, we too must wait—sometimes for a long time. There is the patience of prayer as well as the restlessness of prayer.

Emil Brunner has observed that prayer is much more difficult than ordinary work and much more exhausting. "For a hundred men who are not afraid of the exertion of labor, there are only a few who take upon themselves the strain of prayer." This is not surprising, since "it requires an effort of the will,—and more than that. 'I will arise and go to my Father.' That resolution requires the courage to let God tell you the truth, the humiliating knowledge that you can no longer help yourself."[17]

Marshall McLuhan, Roman Catholic layman, in an address to the 27th annual convention of the National Religious Broadcasters in Washington, D.C. (1970), surprised his listeners by suggesting that "prayer is violence."[18] It is a "special kind of violence," for it consists in "banging and slamming on the gates of heaven until they open." He also made clear that prayer is the violence that cures, because through prayer we are delivered from our inward misery and fear.

I have emphasized the rightful place for struggle and importunity in prayer, but there is also a time to cease from the struggle. We can knock at the door of God's heaven, but we cannot force the hand of God. We are not to reject what is plainly his will, we are to desist when his will becomes clear to us. A woman whom I know prayed that her dying mother might live, and she refused to take no for an answer. God heeded her request, but her mother was left paralyzed. She would not accept her mother's death, and consequently had to devote her time almost exclusively to the care of her mother for many years afterwards.

To surrender and submit to God's will is also a work of faith, and sometimes it is more difficult than striving with God. Sibbes observes, "It is as hard a matter to suffer God's will as to do his will. Passive obedience is as hard as active."[19] One must now struggle against one's own will and put to death one's own desires.

We should pray for discernment in our prayers. It may be God's will that we keep on praying, but it may also be his will that we submit and obey. The only way to find out is to keep praying until his will becomes certain to us. We should generally not act until we are confident that God has given us a definite answer.

True prayer entails a strategy. I concur with Hallesby that "the labor of prayer requires a definite plan and purpose."[20] We should pray in such a way that God's kingdom might be advanced, that God's glory might be magnified, that God's will and purpose might be done.

Prayer is both a stepping stone to Christian service and the culmination of Christian service. It must not be practiced to the exclusion of works of mercy. Such works are also forms of Christian service, and indeed necessary forms.

Prayer that does not bear fruit in self-giving service is not Christian prayer but only soliloquy. Prayer with obedience is power, but without obedience it is presumption. The integral relation between prayer and service is forcefully brought home by that redoubtable prayer warrior Richard Sibbes:

> As for us to pray to God to bless us, and then to do nothing, it is a barren prayer; so to thank God, and then to do nothing, it is a barren thanksgiving. Our deeds have words, our deeds have a voice to God. They speak, they pray. There is a kind of prayer, a kind of thanks in our works.[21]

## ACTION AND CONTEMPLATION

Contemplation (meaning here the life of prayer and devotion) will bear fruit in action, but action in turn will drive us ever again to contemplation. Moltmann expresses my own sentiments on this question:

> Just as meditation cannot be a flight from action, so, conversely, action cannot be a flight from meditation. Anyone who falls back on activity because he cannot come to terms with himself, and who praises action because he is afraid of theory, achieves nothing at all, but is merely a burden to other people.[22]

Jesus was exceptionally busy, often having no leisure even for meals (Mark 6:31, GNB). But he did not sacrifice his prayer time. The demands upon him became a call to devote extra time to prayer (Mark 1:32–35; Luke 5:15, 16; John 6:15). Sometimes our Lord prayed inwardly even when the disciples were with him (Luke 9:18). On occasion he withdrew from the crowds who were seeking to be healed (Luke 5:15, 16). He advised his disciples, "Come away by yourselves to a lonely place, and rest a while" (Mark 6:31).

Meister Eckhart, as a true mystic, saw the preeminent value of contemplation, but the evangelical or biblical side of his theology was evident in his firm commitment to mission and service to others. Surprisingly, he could assert: "In contemplation, you serve only yourself. In good works, you serve many people."[23] He perceived that the unity that one beholds in contemplation inevitably leads to subsequent works of mercy: "What we plant in the soil of contemplation we shall reap in the harvest of action and thus the purpose of contemplation is achieved."[24]

Christian prayer will invariably give rise to activity that seeks the fulfillment of the prayer request. We do not pray in earnest if we do not commit ourselves to do our best to bring about what we hope and pray for. There is no prayer without risk. We must take the risk of becoming involved in the action of prayer. We cannot, for example, pray for racial peace without extending the hand of friendship to members of a minority race and also supporting legislation that insures their civil rights.

Yet we should always keep in mind that we in ourselves do not bring about the answer. We can contribute to the answer, but even then not apart from the Spirit of God. Prayer is not bound to the humanly possible. We must be involved in what we request, but the key to success lies in the power and action of God.

Mary and Martha, the two sisters of Bethany, are commonly held up as representative of the contemplative and active lives respectively (Luke 10:38–42). While Mary listened to the words of Jesus, Martha was busy in the kitchen preparing the meal. It is interesting to note that Eckhart regarded Martha more highly than Mary, because in his opinion the former had already achieved contemplation and was now sharing the fruits of her faith and love. Teresa of Avila spoke favorably of both Martha and Mary. The mainstream of Christian spirituality upholds Mary over Martha, and here I include Bernard, Thomas Aquinas, Luther, Sibbes, and the author of *The Cloud of Unknowing*. It is important to understand that Mary was not engaged in meditation or mental prayer but in hearing the Word of God. Moreover, our text plainly tells us that "the part that Mary has chosen is best; and it shall not be taken away from her" (Luke 10:42, NEB; cf. Luke 11:28).

While contemplation has a certain priority over service to our neighbor, such service is the cardinal evidence and consequence of a life of devotion. The highest form of service, moreover, is the apostolate, telling others the good news of God's great work of reconciliation and redemption. The psalmist declares, "But for me it is good to be near God; I have made the Lord God my refuge, that I may tell of all thy works" (Ps. 73:28).

Thomas Aquinas, revealing here a decided evangelical stance, affirmed that the mixed or apostolic life is the most excellent. It is to be ranked over contemplation per se, but it must be grounded in contemplation. As he put it, "Even as it is better to enlighten than merely to shine, so is it better to give to others the fruits of one's contemplation than merely to contemplate."[25] Thus, "to labor for the salvation of our neighbor, even at the expense of contemplation, for the love of God and neighbor, appears to be a higher perfection of charity than if he would cling so dearly to the sweetness of contemplation as to be totally unwilling to sacrifice it even for the salvation of others."[26]

Besides preaching and teaching, the prayer of intercession forms a major part of the task of the apostolate. It is not enough to share the good news: we must also pray that people might open their hearts to the gospel. It is not enough to preach to souls; we must also win souls for the kingdom through intercessory prayer. St. Mary of Jesus, a Carmelite nun, has rightly said, "It is the prayer of agony which saves the world."[27]

## VARIOUS TYPES OF DISCIPLESHIP

It can be shown that the real activists have been the contemplatives. I am thinking here not of mystical contemplation so much as commitment to the life of prayer and devotion. Yet this does not imply that all contemplatives have been activists. It does indicate that creative action in the world entails contemplation in the sense of conscious and continual communion with God. There must be "an intake of divine light into the soul" before there can be a "pouring out" of this light upon the world.[28]

The lives of the great saints of the church testify that inward devotion to Christ and a life of prayer have a revolutionary impact upon society and history. John Chrysostom, who dedicated himself to a life of prayer and preaching, courageously raised his voice against social injustices: he denounced the inhumane treatment of slaves and deplored the pursuit of luxury by Christians in high places in a time when most people lived in dire poverty. Although his intention was only to live a solitary monastic life, Bernard of Clairvaux became a notable public figure, a reformer of the church, an adversary of heretics, and a coun-

selor to kings and popes. Almost singlehandedly he stopped po-
groms against the Jews in western Germany and spearheaded
the Second Crusade, whose object was to free the Holy Land
from infidels. Catherine of Siena, after spending several years of
her life in mystical seclusion in one of the rooms in her father's
house, emerged to become one of the great political personages
of her day; popes and heads of state sought her advice as she
tried to bring peace between the insurgent Italian cities and to
restore the papacy to Rome.

Protestant saints likewise planted the seeds of cultural
change and social reform. John Calvin, who lived in simplicity
and died in virtual poverty, united a life of prayer, study, and
devotion with intense political involvement, remaking the city
of Geneva into a holy community which functioned as a refuge
for the victims of religious persecution (though admittedly not
all refugees were welcome). Marguerite of Navarre (d. 1549),
French Huguenot queen, who daily walked with God, promoted
education and opened half a dozen hospitals in her tiny moun-
tain kingdom near the Spanish border. While always seeking to
cultivate inner communion with his God, Jonathan Edwards
went out of his way to speak out against unethical business
practices and to defend Indian land rights. In his sermons and
pamphlets John Wesley took vigorous stands on poverty and
riches, sea piracy, smuggling, and the slave trade. After a long
period of isolation in prayer and contemplation, the Reformed
mystic Gerhard Tersteegen became an open-air preacher and
famed curer of souls. His witness and writings posed a threat to
the state church as well as a challenge to the war policy of his
nation. In 1740 local pastors succeeded in persuading the au-
thorities to impose a ban on his meetings; for ten years Tersteegen was prohibited from preaching the gospel in Protestant
Germany.

In the contemporary period, too, we see the crucial role of
prayer and devotion in the lives of Christian heroes and confes-
sors, those who have made a definite impact upon both the
church and world. Martin Luther King gained strength and

courage to carry on the civil rights struggle through prayer and
Bible study as well as active participation in black gospel ser-
vices. Although her chief concern was the spreading of the gospel, Corrie Ten Boom found herself involved in political subver-
sion following the Nazi conquest of Holland. Participating in an
underground ring that forged papers for Jews and hid Jews from
their Nazi oppressors, she was imprisoned first in her own country and then in Germany. After the war, she established a half-
way house for concentration camp victims and embarked on a
career as a traveling evangelist. Archbishop Helder Camara of
Brazil, a man of deep prayer and devotion, has gained a worldwide reputation as a champion of the dispossessed. He has spoken out forcefully against the torture of political prisoners and
other acts of political repression in his country and throughout
Latin America. As a result, he has been threatened with physical violence, his books have been banned, and he has been reduced to the status of a "nonperson" in his native land. Surely
Karl Barth, too, should be cited as one who bore witness to
Christ in the midst of the world's anguish; leading the struggle
of the Confessing Church against National Socialism, he had a
decisive influence on the church and world of his day through
his writings, letters, sermons, and lectures.

Not all those who embrace either an apostolic or a contemplative life, of course, have been directly involved in the political
turmoils of their times. Yet, through their prayers and intercessions and also through their spiritual counsel, they have nonetheless exerted an indirect and sometimes pervasive influence
on politics and culture.

It can be shown that the saints and mystics of the church, including the luminaries of Puritanism and Pietism, have fur-
nished the inspiration for the great missionary enterprises of
the church.[29] Catholic missions have been carried on by the
great religious orders, including contemplative orders, while
Protestant missions are the fruit of the evangelical awakenings.

The following story (which may be more apocryphal than fac-
tual) illustrates the need for both prayer and service, and the

complementarity of contemplative and active styles of life. A delegation of Protestant ministers was visiting the hospital and school of one of the Catholic sisterhoods and expressed its admiration for what it observed. The ministers made clear that the kinds of nuns they respected were the active ones who were always busy teaching and serving. The mother superior had to remind them that the works of selfless service they witnessed were made possible partly because of the prayer support the active nuns received from their contemplative sisters who were living in virtual seclusion in a convent on the hill. While we must acknowledge that prayer and devotion take precedence over service per se, we must not infer from this story that contemplative monastics are more praiseworthy than sisters of mercy who also engage in prayer and worship. Indeed, contemplation becomes self-defeating unless it clearly serves and promotes the missionary proclamation and the ministry of mercy in the world.

The priority of devotion and prayer over the predominantly active or secular life is attested in Exodus 17:8–13. Moses was on the hill with two lieutenants, Aaron and Hur, with his hands raised in prayer. Down in the plain, Joshua and his army were locked in battle with the pagan Amalekites. Although he was far removed from the tangible enemy, Moses through his prayers turned the tide of the battle. Oswald Sanders makes this astute comment: "The seeming inactivity of prayer on the hill proved to be a greater test of spiritual stamina than fighting in the valley. It was Moses who tired, not Joshua."[30]

Every Christian life should be nurtured by prayer and should bear fruit in works of love. As we have seen, contemplation and action are organically related, and the life of faith should always include both facets.

At this point it is appropriate to consider whether there is a place for vocations to prayer. Is it biblical to devote oneself exclusively to the life of contemplation? Olive Wyon advances the view that "some people may even be called, as in times past, to live permanently in partial retirement, in order that, as 'guardians of the spirit,' they may continually bring fresh streams of

Eternity into time."[31] I too see the place for contemplative vocations so long as those who embrace them live in fellowship with and accountability to their more active brothers and sisters in the world. As an evangelical Protestant, I also insist that those who are called to this particular pattern of discipleship not see themselves as embracing a higher kind of existence or spirituality. The two patterns of discipleship are not subordinate to one another but complementary. Both involve the continual practice of prayer, though one is devoted exclusively to prayer and devotion, while the other combines prayer and self-giving service.

Perpetual isolation or total retirement from the world is unbiblical, since there is no precedent for this in biblical history. Yet the idea of a community dedicated to prayer on behalf of the world and living in constant contact with the crying needs of the world is in accord with the deepest intuitions of biblical faith. Forsyth has affirmed that "it is truer to say that we live the Christian life in order to pray than that we pray in order to live the Christian life."[32] The life devoted to prayer, study and meditation is not higher on the scale of merit, but in certain periods of the church's history it may be more necessary, particularly when worldliness has eroded the spiritual life of the church.

Prayer in the Christian sense does not remove us from the world but enables us to see the world in the perspective of God's plan and purpose for it. According to Thomas Merton, prayer "transforms our vision of the world, and makes us see it . . . in the light of God."[33] Those who pray in the biblical way become more sensitive to the crying needs of the world, both spiritual and material, and are moved to alleviate these needs. Contemplatives in a cloister meet these needs through their prayers of intercession and also through the refuge they provide for world-weary Christians seeking periodic retreat and inward renewal. Through their newsletters, magazines, books, and letters, contemplatives can engage in a powerful ministry of evangelism.

There are two basic kinds of discipleship, though these are

sometimes combined in various ways. The first is characterized by retirement from the world and the second by active service in the world. The first entails a literal renunciation of family, property, and marriage and sometimes also participation in government so that one can be free to devote oneself wholly to the apostolate of prayer. In the second pattern of discipleship, one seeks to realize his apostolic vocation while engaged in secular pursuits. Here money, property, and family become a means to glorify God and advance his kingdom in the world. Both types of discipleship entail inward renunciation of self and of anything that stands in the way of God.

Each pattern of discipleship has its peculiar temptations and dangers. The eremitic and monastic ways are constantly threatened by a false kind of mysticism in which one's attention is turned away from the anguish of the world to the vision of God. The call to the cloister is also bedeviled by Pharisaism, in which one falls into the delusion that one is making oneself morally acceptable to God and therefore superior to the ordinary Christian. Closely related are the pitfalls of legalism, where monastic works are made a condition for salvation, and of rigorism, in which strictness of living is deemed necessary to arrive at life's spiritual goal. We need to remind ourselves that Jesus preferred generosity of spirit to the scrupulous regard for the canons of piety and that he claimed as his friends the poor and despised of the world, not the religiously zealous or morally good. Monasticism as its best, however, reminds us that no sacrifice is too great for the one who is serious about Christian commitment and that the fellowship of sacrificial love that transcends the claims of home and family can be realized in part now as a sign and parable of the coming eschatological kingdom.

The Reformation as well as Puritanism and Pietism placed the emphasis on living the Christian life in the midst of the world's conflict and anguish. Its motto was not flight from the world but the overthrow of the principalities and powers of the world. Its asceticism was an inner-worldly asceticism aimed at bringing the power structures of the world under the guidance and direction of the kingdom of God. Christ was regarded as the transformer of culture who sent his disciples into the world to subdue it, rather than as a spiritual master who called his subjects to live above the life of politics and culture.

The chief danger in the world-oriented discipleship is secularism in which this-worldly goals such as justice and freedom become ends in themselves. Clericalism is indeed another form of secularism, for here the church is transformed into simply another power structure within society. Unless our ethical tasks in the world are anchored in a transcendent meaning and purpose, they are bound to have no higher goal than a just society. Christianity is not mysticism, but a religion that is divorced from its mystical wellsprings becomes a merely moral or humanistic faith.

Discipleship in the world is also liable to succumb to its own form of Pharisaism in which the property owner is regarded as more worthy than the itinerant beggar and the married person with a family more acceptable in the sight of God than the celibate. Bourgeois standards rather than biblical norms constantly intrude into a discipleship in the world. It is well to note that Calvin had a high regard for the calling of celibacy and believed it to have a practical, though not a moral, advantage over marriage.[34]

Out of the tradition of Protestant evangelicalism communities have emerged as centers of spiritual renewal. Among these are the Moravian communities of Herrnhut, Marienborn, Bethlehem, and Salem; the Ephrata cloister founded by Johann Conrad Beissel near Lancaster, Pennsylvania; the community of the Pilgrims' Cottage established under the influence of the Reformed mystic Gerhard Tersteegen; the Dohnavur Fellowship in South India founded by the evangelical missionary Amy Carmichael; the Trevecka community of Howell Harris in Wales; and the Amana Society, known also as the Community of True Inspiration, in Iowa. In our time, we can mention the formation of evangelical monastic sisterhoods and brotherhoods, including the Evangelical Sisterhood of Mary in Darmstadt, Germany; the

Brothers of Taizé in Burgundy, France; the Brotherhood of
Christ in Selbitz, Germany; the Sisters of Pomeyrol in southern
France; the Jesus Brotherhood in Germany; and St. Augustine's
House in Oxford, Michigan. Then there are nonmonastic communities that emphasize the apostolate of preaching and mission as well as prayer: L'Abri Fellowship in Switzerland and England; Lee Abbey and Scargill in England; the Iona community
in Scotland; the Corrymeela community in northern Ireland;
Bethany Fellowship in Minneapolis, Minnesota; Koinonia Farm
in Americus, Georgia; Salem Acres near Freeport, Illinois; the
Reba Place Fellowship in Evanston, Illinois; Jesus Abbey in
South Korea; Living Water Ranch in Oldsburg, Kansas; Christian Outreach Center, a Lutheran charismatic community south
of St. Louis, Missouri; and the Community of Celebration in
Colorado Springs, Colorado. Many others could be mentioned as
added confirmation of a genuine revival in community life in
evangelical Protestantism today.

It is not my purpose here to give a critique of these communities, but it is noteworthy that a discipleship that stresses a return to the contemplative and mystical wellsprings of the faith
is once again becoming a live option for many Christians.[35]
When Christian action becomes activism, then it is time to restore the balance by emphasizing the necessity of the life of
prayer and devotion. But prayer must never be divorced from
mission in the world, just as the study of Scripture and theology
must never be separated from ethics. Those who find themselves called to withdrawal from the pursuits and tumult and
discord in the world for the purpose of deeper communion with
God must see to it that the experiences they attain and the message they now more fully understand are carried back into the
world so that sinners might be converted and the kingdom of
God advanced. In evangelical theology (as in the Bible), withdrawal is always closely associated with return, since prayer has
among its salient goals charitable service and evangelism.

With Thomas Aquinas I agree that the mixed life, that which
combines contemplation and action, is closest to the evangelical

ideal indicated in the Scriptures.[36] Certainly this kind of life is clearly discernible in the biblical prophets and apostles, and most of all in Jesus himself. The mixed life resembles the monastic type of discipleship in that it entails full-time service in fulfilling the apostolic mandate of the church. It is not to be regarded as more meritorious than the common life in the world, but it may well be more important in furthering the work of Christian mission.[37] In Protestantism, this kind of discipleship is exemplified in foreign missionaries, especially those involved in faith missions; full-time staff of student service organizations such as the InterVarsity Christian Fellowship; members of deaconess sisterhoods; pastors of local congregations; full-time teachers of the Christian faith in mission schools and seminaries; officers in the Salvation Army and in paraparochial organizations like the Church Army; rescue mission workers; itinerant evangelists (such as the Methodist Circuit Riders); and members of evangelical missionary orders such as the Navigators, the Wycliffe Bible Translators, the Worldwide Evangelization Crusade, Operation Mobilization, the St. Chrischona Pilgrim Mission, and Bethany Fellowship.

I also concur with Thomas Aquinas that the contemplative life, which focuses on study, prayer, and meditation, has a certain precedence over the purely active life. Those who embrace a contemplative vocation must be concerned that their contemplation bear fruit in the lives of others and serve the missionary mandate of the church. Those Christians who enter into a fully secular occupation must take the time to give their work meaning and direction by drawing constantly near to God in prayer and by immersing themselves in God's Word as given in Scripture and the preaching of the church.

## AN AGE OF ACTIVISM

The technological society in which we live spurns contemplation and idealizes action. But activity that is divorced from contemplation becomes busyness, which is in effect the new holiness. The two virtues of the technological society are utility and efficiency. A demand for results governs both the secular and religious life of modern man. Religion is valued mainly for the service that it renders to society. The people most highly regarded are producers, not thinkers, and much less pray-ers. It is supposed that no problem is beyond the reach of technology, that no mystery defies an adequate human resolution.

In this context prayer becomes a means for getting things done. Its success is measured by its efficacy as determined by the canons of scientific rationality. Whereas its primary aim should be to serve God's glory and prepare the way for his kingdom, it is now reduced to a formula for achieving goals that are prized by the secular culture. Thomas Merton complains that "prayer tends to lose its true character in so far as it becomes busy, full of ulterior purposes, and committed to programs that are beneath its own level."[38] Work itself is seen as a form of prayer, perhaps the highest form; thus we have the misleading motto "To work is to pray."

Under the spell of a technocratic liberalism, the church has been misled into thinking that it could bring in the kingdom of God by social engineering. Secular humanism has invaded the citadels of the faith itself, and the horizontal dimension of existence—that is, our relationship with our fellow human beings— has crowded out the vertical dimension, our relationship with God. We should heed Solzhenitsyn's words of wisdom in his celebrated Harvard University address (spring 1978): "We have placed too much hope in political and social reforms, only to find out that we were being deprived of our most precious possession: our spiritual life."[39]

In order to counter the prevailing mood, we must stress again the priority of being over acting. Before we can engage in meaningful service in the world, we need to be in communion with the living God and gain the knowledge of his favor as seen in Jesus Christ. Before we can do deeds that are truly characterized by grace and mercy, we need to be in a state of grace. "In the life of grace and sanctification," said Sibbes, "there is a power and

ability to believe in God, and to be holy, and to love God; and
... the actions of love spring from that power."[40]

The great saints of the church were often activists, but their
activity was grounded in and informed by prayer. Luther once
acknowledged that one day he had so much to do that he had to
spend four hours in prayer in order to get everything finished.
The greater our responsibilities in the world, the more crucial
and necessary is the practice of prayer.

Work is not necessarily prayer, but prayer is always work. Indeed, it is the greatest work, the highest work possible for a
Christian. Prayer should command the full attention of the
Christian and engage his or her whole being; yet it can have
power and meaning only through the intervention of the Holy
Spirit into the life of the Christian. To participate in the salvation of Christ through prayer and to abide in mystical communion with him is a divine work, for it can be accomplished only
through the Spirit of God.

Prayer is the key to confidence, boldness, and revival for the
individual Christian and for the church as a whole. Lorenzo
Scupoli has rightly said,

> Every thought which discourages and hinders thee from increasing
> in love and confidence towards God is a messenger of hell. . . . Thou
> must drive it away, and neither admit it nor give it a hearing. For the
> office of the Holy Spirit is none other than always and on all occa-
> sions to unite the soul more and more closely to God, enkindling and
> inflaming it with His sweet love, and inspiring it with fresh confi-
> dence.[41]

There is a timidity and caution in too much Christian prayer.
We pray for individuals but not for nations, we pray for the sur-
vival of the church but not for the transformation of the world.
Obedience is not mere resignation or submission: it entails taking up the sword of the Lord and slaying the dragon that para-
lyzes the church and world today. I agree with Luther that when
a person confesses his sins, "he must not think that he can put
down his burden and live quietly, but he must know that by

putting down his burden he becomes a soldier of God and thereby assumes another burden, namely, to fight for God against the devil and his own faults."[42]

The opposite of an aimless activism is not quietism but creative action, action with meaning and purpose, action that is anchored in the transcendent and directed to it. We need to rediscover the roots of true action in contemplation. We need to rekindle the fire that is already resident within us through the indwelling Holy Spirit and set the world on fire with the flame of the gospel. What is needed in a technological age is the contagion of the fire of the Holy Spirit that will make the church again a Pentecostal fellowship; only this kind of church can turn the world upside down (cf. Acts 17:6).

## NOTES

1. Søren Kierkegaard, *Journals,* ed. and trans. Alexander Dru (London: Oxford University Press, 1951), 588, p. 158.
2. P. T. Forsyth, *The Soul of Prayer,* 5th ed. (London: Independent Press, 1966), p. 28.
3. The not uncommon mystical denigration of action in the world is reflected in this remark of the English hermit, Richard Rolle: "Those contemplatives who are most on fire with the love of eternity . . . never, or scarcely ever, engage in outside activity . . . They tend to keep themselves to themselves, ever ready to reach up to Christ with joyful song"—Richard Rolle, *The Fire of Love,* trans. Clifton Wolters (London: Penguin Books, 1972), p. 53.
4. Forsyth, *The Soul of Prayer,* p. 11.
5. John Calvin, *Sermons on the Epistle to the Ephesians* (Edinburgh: Banner of Truth Trust, 1975), p. 682.
6. Ladislaus Boros, *Meeting God in Man,* trans. William Glen-Doepel (Garden City, N.Y.: Doubleday, 1971), p. 39.
7. *Apophthegms of the Fathers,* J.-P. Migne, *Patrologia Graeca,* 65, 112 B. Cited in Ellul, *Prayer and Modern Man,* trans. C. Edward Hopkin (New York: Seabury Press, 1970), p. 139.
8. *Luther, Lectures on Romans,* ed. and trans. Wm. Pauck (Philadelphia: Westminster Press, 1961), p. 349.
9. Karl Barth, *Church Dogmatics,* Vol. II, 1, p. 511.
10. Cited in Heiler, *Prayer,* trans. and ed. Samuel McComb (New York: Oxford University Press, 1958), p. 263.
11. Richard Sibbes, *Complete Works,* Vol. 1, p. 66.

12. Forsyth, *The Soul of Prayer,* p. 62.
13. Cited in Oswald Sanders, *Prayer Power Unlimited* (Chicago: Moody Press, 1977), p. 132.
14. Sibbes, *Complete Works,* Vol. 1, p. 265.
15. Andrew Murray, *With Christ in the School of Prayer* (Westwood, N.J.: Revell, 1966), p. 8.
16. Hallesby, *Prayer,* trans. Clarence Carlsen (Minneapolis: Augsburg, 1931), p. 98. Despite Hallesby's awareness of struggle in the life of prayer, the quietist, mystical element is more dominant than the evangelical one in his spirituality. Too often it seems that for him the struggle is not an anguished cry but a painless surrender. The work of the Spirit is so emphasized that human endeavor seems small in comparison. Prayer for Hallesby is more a friendly colloquy than an unceasing battle. Although he speaks of wrestling in prayer, he makes clear that we wrestle not with God but with ourselves, with the distractions of the world. Admittedly, he does make a place for wrestling with the powers of darkness. He emphasizes too much our helplessness, clinging to God in our weakness and not also in our strength. Moreover, God's love is stressed almost to the exclusion of his holiness. The essence of prayer for Hallesby is "an attitude of our hearts towards God," a "holy passivity."
17. Emil Brunner, *Our Faith,* trans. John W. Rilling (New York: Scribner's, 1954), p. 117.
18. Cited in *The Presbyterian Journal,* 28, no. 42 (1970), p. 4.
19. Sibbes, *Complete Works,* Vol. 1, p. 403.
20. Hallesby, *Prayer,* p. 82.
21. Sibbes, *Complete Works,* Vol. 3, p. 201.
22. Jürgen Moltmann, *The Church in the Power of the Spirit,* trans. Margaret Kohl (New York: Harper & Row, 1977), p. 285.
23. Meister Eckhart, *Meister Eckhart,* ed. and trans. Raymond Blakney (New York: Harper, 1941), p. 111.
24. *Ibid.*
25. Thomas Aquinas, *Summa Theologica* II-II ae. Q. 188 Art. 6 (New York: Benziger, 1947), p. 1999.
26. Thomas Aquinas, *De Perfectione Vitae Spiritualis,* cited in Martin Grabmann, *The Interior Life of St. Thomas Aquinas* (Milwaukee: Bruce 1951), p. 40.
27. *A Carmelite of the Sacred Heart,* trans. M. E. Arendrug (New York: Benziger, 1923), p. 125.
28. Leon Cristiani, *St. Bernard of Clairvaux,* trans. M. Angeline Bouchard (Boston: Daughters of St. Paul, 1977), p. 47.
29. Needless to say, not all mystics have been in the forefront of missions. Only those whose spirituality has been drawn from the wellsprings of biblical faith have become involved in the evangelistic mandate.

The "saints and mystics of the church" in this context includes prophetic figures whose mysticism has been qualified and purified by the claims of biblical faith. It excludes those mystics whose loyalty has been to the broader religious community rather than to the church, and even more to the gospel that created the church, and who have been prone to place their own experiences over the teachings of both Scripture and the church. Radical mysticism means the dissolution of the church as well as th⌐ renunciation of culture.

30. Sanders, *Prayer Power Unlimited*, p. 152.

31. Olive Wyon, *The School of Prayer*, 2d ed. (New York: Macmillan, 1966), p. 187. She acknowledges her indebtedness to Karl Mannheim at this point.

32. Forsyth, *The Soul of Prayer*, p. 16.

33. Thomas Merton, *Contemplative Prayer* (Garden City, N.Y.: Doubleday/Image Books, 1971), p. 112.

34. Among evangelical saints who heeded the call to celibacy were Andrew Melville, Richard Sibbes, Isaac Watts, Francis Asbury, William Law, Gerhard Tersteegen, Evangeline Booth, Amy Carmichael, John Hyde, and Søren Kierkegaard. In our own time, we can mention Corrie Ten Boom, J. Gresham Machen, Max Thurian of Taizé, and Klara Schlink, founder of the Evangelical Sisterhood of Mary. There are others who, though married, have embraced a vocation to apostolic poverty: George Müller of the Plymouth Brethren; Clarence Jordan of the Koinonia Farm community; George Verwer, founder of Operation Mobilization; Eberhard Arnold of the Society of Brothers; and Walter and Hanna Hümmer, founders of the Brotherhood of Christ.

35. See Donald G. Bloesch, *Wellsprings of Renewal* (Grand Rapids, Mich.: Eerdmans, 1974); Olive Wyon, *Living Springs* (Philadelphia: Westminster Press, 1962); Dave and Neta Jackson, *Living Together in a World Falling Apart* (Carol Stream, Ill.: Creation House, 1974); and Charles A. Fracchia, *Living Together Alone: The New American Monasticism* (New York: Harper & Row, 1979). For a constant update on new ventures in Protestant community life, see *Sojourners* magazine.

36. This is not to deny that in periods of extreme spiritual dearth when the very citadels of the church are invaded by worldliness, contemplative vocations may be more necessary even than those which unite prayer and service in the world. The church, including the evangelical church, ever needs the monastery as a sign of God's new order that stands over against the powers and structures of the world.

My understanding of the "mixed life" includes a greater diversity of ministries than Thomas envisioned, but I am in agreement that the full-time apostolate is the representative pattern of this kind of discipleship.

37. This is not to underestimate the manifest opportunities for Christian witness on the part of those who choose to live out their Christian vocations while engaged in secular tasks. We need only think of Christians in the field of politics who are in a position to ensure that the rules that govern society at large are brought into ever closer harmony with God's commandments.

38. Merton, *Contemplative Prayer*, p. 114.

39. See James M. Wall, "Solzhenitsyn's Harvard Sermon," *The Christian Century*, 95, no. 29 (1978): 843.

40. Sibbes, *Complete Works*, Vol. 4, p. 258.
41. Lorenzo Scupoli, *The Spiritual Combat* (London: Burns, Oates & Washbourne, 1935), p. 266.
42. *Luther: Lectures on Romans*, p. 212.

# VIII

# The Goal of Prayer

## TWO UNDERSTANDINGS

When we consider the goal of prayer, we are again confronted with two quite different understandings that are conspicuous throughout Christian history: mysticism and biblical personalism. While the mystics generally envision the goal of the Christian life as possession of God, evangelical religion sees it primarily as fellowship with God and with all the saints. Mysticism following Plato and Plotinus emphasizes the beatific vision of God. Evangelical faith, on the other hand, stresses the sovereignty of God: this means that the most important thing is obedience to God's will, not the contemplation of his being.

Yet, before we make this distinction too sharp, we should recall that there is a mystical element in biblical faith itself which speaks of the beholding of God in wonder and love. In Psalm 27 (v. 8), we read, "Thou hast said, 'Seek ye my face.' My heart says to thee, 'Thy face, Lord, do I seek.' " Psalm 63 declares: "O God, you are my God, and I long for you. My whole being desires you.... Let me see how mighty and glorious you are.... My soul will feast and be satisfied" (Ps. 63:1, 2, 5, GNB; cf. Ps. 42:1, 2). Moses is described as beholding the form of God (Num. 12:8), and Paul speaks of seeing God "face to face" in the eschatological fulness of time (1 Cor. 13:12).

The great evangelical movements of the Reformation, Pietism

and Puritanism, also occasionally employed the language of vision and union in depicting the goal of life's pilgrimage. Richard Sibbes could say, "So to know God in Christ, labour to see the face of God in Christ."[1] Yet for Sibbes and other Puritans this meant that we should seek the loving presence of God, the favor of God as revealed in Jesus Christ, which is already available to us. The eschatological goal can be anticipated now in repentance and faith. Through faith we can even now be united with Christ, but we do not yet see this union. It is hidden from us, but it will be revealed on the last day.[2]

When biblical, prophetic religion employs the language of union, it does not have in mind becoming one with the being of God or being absorbed into the abysmal nature of God, as in monistic mysticism. In the biblical passages just cited, the focus is on intimate communion with God, not fusion with God in the Platonic or Neo-Platonic sense. The vision of God that Paul speaks of in 1 Corinthians 13:12 is a full understanding of God's will and purpose and unhampered fellowship with him, not a perpetual ecstatic gazing upon the being of God. The biblical Christian strives not for deification in the sense of transformation into God but sanctification, meaning an increasing conformity of the human will to the will of God. Our aim is to be elevated not to the level of deity but to the realm or state where there is perfect fellowship with deity.

Prophetic, biblical religion must not be confused with an ethical religion that denies or underplays the pivotal place of the adoration of God in the life of the Christian. Service of our neighbor does not have priority over the service of God's glory, but it is the vital fruit and evidence of a living faith and devotion to a holy God.

God is not simply a means to the fulfillment of humanity, but humanity finds its fulfillment only in the glory of God. We love God because of who he is and what he has done, not simply in order to procure his gifts. That kind of utilitarianism is foreign to prophetic religion at its best and bears a much closer resemblance to primitive religion.

There is an appreciative love of God as well as a self-giving love toward our neighbor. This is not simply natural love transformed but supernatural love returned to its Giver. As biblical Christians, we seek the beholding of the glory of God as well as the manifestation of this glory in the world. We seek our salvation in God as well as the salvation of the world for God. Some of those who have been particularly vehement in their criticisms of Christian mysticism (such as Nygren and Ozment) have failed to do justice to those biblical passages that speak of the union or intimate communion of the soul with God. When Jesus is portrayed as the vine and the members of his church as the branches (John 15:5), this is surely a graphic way of describing the intimate union of the believer with his Savior, a union that has been realized in faith, as both Calvin and Luther freely acknowledged. Though already united with God through faith in Christ, we need to confirm and deepen this union through adoring and self-sacrificing love.

The Song of Songs has played a key role in the bridal mysticism that was so prevalent in the later Middle Ages and that reappeared in Pietism and Puritanism. What is unfortunate in this kind of piety is that our love for Christ is often treated as a spiritualized form of Eros, and the radical uniqueness of Christian love as Agape, self-serving as over against self-regarding love, is lost sight of. One commentator says of Bernard of Clairvaux's sermons on the Song of Songs: "Human love is only a roughcast of true love, the love of God for us and of a human soul for its God."[3] For Bernard, sensual or carnal love is but one stage leading first to intellectual love and then to spiritual love. I contend that Agape love does not simply fulfill Eros, but challenges it—indeed, calls it into question, particularly as a pathway to redemption. At the same time, it does not totally annul Eros but instead transforms it so that it is made to serve that higher love which places the glory of God above human happiness and fulfillment.

The mystics were not mistaken in seeking to relate the sexual love of the Song of Songs to the supernatural love between God and the soul or God and the church. Sexuality has its basis in the deep-felt yearnings of the soul for God. Sexual love is not merely biological, for when it is united with Agape love, it can be seen as a reflection of God's love for his people and of the human response to this love. The allegorists were not altogether wrong, since the Song of Songs itself contains hints of the role of supernatural powers in the act of love.[4]

The right way to use the Song of Songs is to begin with God's revelation of himself in Jesus Christ and then to see the Song of Songs in light of this redemptive act. Beginning with human love and then trying to find in it the key that opens the doorway to divine love only ends in a false mysticism.

In Ephesians 5:23–33 Paul speaks of Christ's love for his church as analogous to the husband's love for his wife. But Paul is speaking of a Christian marriage, a marriage in the Lord, not of marriage as such. It is important to recognize that Christian marriage is qualitatively different from pagan marriage (cf. 1 Cor. 7:29), because in the former the self-regarding love of Eros is subordinated to the other-regarding love of Agape. We seek to possess the partner in love for the sake of the happiness of the partner, not first of all for our own enjoyment or satisfaction.

It is possible to speak of possessing God as a bride seeks to possess her bridegroom, but the motivation must be the service and happiness of the bridegroom before our own happiness. In our desire for union and fellowship with God, we seek not to control or gain power over him but to gain assurance of his love and of his abiding faithfulness. We seek to possess not his power or glory but instead the reality of what he has promised—the remission of sins and regeneration. And our primary goal in all of this is not to transcend creaturehood in union with divinity but to glorify God as reborn sinners who frankly recognize our creatureliness and helplessness apart from God's grace.

The Pietists and Puritans frequently used the imagery of bridal mysticism in order to underline the intimacy of the union with God that faith accomplishes. There is indeed a mystical note in their writings, but at the same time there is often a marked qualification of mysticism, since the union is always one of will, not of being, and it is based always on grace, never on merit. This is clearly brought out in Christian Keymann's moving hymn *Jesus Will I Never Leave* (seventeenth century), particularly the second verse:

> He is mine, and I am His,
>    Joined with Him in close communion;
> And His bitter passion is
>    The foundation of this union;
> Full of hopes which never yield,
>    Firm on Him, my Rock, I build.[5]

Here we see the convergence of the Savior mysticism of Augustine and Bernard and the prophetic piety of the Reformation, but the latter is dominant. The emphasis is on the union of *faith*, not the ecstatic future union of perfected *love*. The foundation of this union, moreover, is the vicarious atonement of Jesus Christ, not the works of love of the believer. Our hope is anchored in the historical revelation and mediation of Jesus Christ, not in the presence of Eternity within the depths of the soul.

## ULTIMATE AND PENULTIMATE GOALS

The ultimate goal of the life of prayer is the glorification of God and the advancement of his kingdom. Indeed, kingdom service is precisely what gives glory to God. To pray that the glory of God might be made manifest among people in the world is to pray for the fulfillment of God's highest will. It means to pray for the dawning of a new age, when all people may come to know the reality and sovereignty of God (Isa. 66:18; Phil. 2:10, 11; 1 Pet. 4:11).

In evangelical Christianity the aim in true prayer is not to have our own way but to magnify and uphold the Word of God in our lives. Our goal is that the Father might be glorified in the Son throughout the world (John 14:13).

World evangelization is to be numbered among the primary goals in prayer, since the proclaiming of the gospel is what gives glory to God. Paul urged the Thessalonians to "pray for us, that the word of the Lord may speed on and triumph, as it did among you" (2 Thess. 3:1). And, in Luther's words, "Christians ... who love Christ sincerely, have no greater desire and purpose than to see God's kingdom promoted, His name and honor proclaimed and extolled, and His will carried out by everyone."[6] This evangelistic note is also readily discernible in Richard Sibbes: "After we are gained to Christ ourselves, we should labour to gain others to Christ."[7]

Besides the ultimate goals in prayer, there are penultimate goals, which are valid but nevertheless subordinate to advancing the glory of God and the kingdom of God. "We pray," says Calvin, "to the glory of God. We ask first for what only serves His glory, and then for whatever serves our well-being."[8]

Certainly our own salvation is a worthy goal in prayer, though it should always be seen as a means to the glory of God. In a time when it is considered egocentric to be concerned about one's own salvation, we would do well to heed these words of Jonathan Edwards: "This seeking eternal life should not only be one concern that our souls are taken up about with other things; but salvation should be sought as the one thing needful ... as the one thing that is desired."[9]

Not only salvation but preservation in this world is a worthy goal in prayer. It is not wrong to seek protection from the powers of death, hell, and sickness, for it is God's will that none of his people should perish (Pss. 37:28; 64:1; 121:7, 8; Matt. 10:29–31; 1 Thess. 5:23; 2 Tim. 4:18). Neither is it wrong to pray for the satisfaction of material needs so long as this does not become the paramount concern in prayer. The mystics constantly frowned on asking for material things and recommended that we "ask nothing of God save God himself" (Augustine). In his interpretation of the Lord's Prayer, Origen considered it a misunderstanding to suppose that we are to pray for material bread: instead, we should pray for the spiritual food that leads to eternal life.[10] As I see it, we should not seek anything higher than what is given to us in Jesus Christ, but we can pray for earthly blessings as well as spiritual blessings so long as they are used in the service of the kingdom. To be sure, union with Christ is the one thing needful; only he is our priceless treasure, and no other blessings or rewards can compare with the peace and joy of being united with him in faith. It is in this light that we can understand these words of Calvin's: "If we have faith we must not seek anything more than Jesus Christ, but he must be all our treasure, because in him we have all things that are necessary for our joy and contentment."[11]

The gifts of the Spirit are also valid objects of prayer. It is true that if we have the Holy Spirit we will also have his gifts, at least potentially, but this does not mean that his gifts are yet manifest in our lives. Among the gifts that are especially necessary for a victorious Christian life are perfect love, fortitude, wisdom, humility, inner peace, and radiant joy (cf. Isa. 11:1–3; Gal. 5:16 ff.; Phil. 4:4–7; 2 Tim. 3:10; 1 Pet. 5:5). Certainly boldness in faith, particularly important in the work of witnessing, is also a gift that every Christian should seek.

Those who are called to be public witnesses to the gospel message of reconciliation, those who are engaged in the ministry of the Word and sacraments, or in itinerant evangelism, need to pray for a special anointing or unction of the Holy Spirit, apart from which their preaching will be bland and powerless. Preaching, like teaching, leadership, miracles and prophecy, is a charismatic gift of the Spirit to be used for the upbuilding of the body of Christ (cf. Isa. 61:1, 2; 1 Cor. 1:17, 2:1–5; 12:27–30; Eph. 4:11, 12; 1 Tim. 4:13, 14; 2 Tim. 1:6, 7, 11). A sermon may have sound exegesis and be properly related to the cultural situation, but if it lacks spiritual fervor, it is still not an evangelical sermon. Edward Bounds wisely observes:

> This unction is not an inalienable gift. It is a conditional gift, and its presence is perpetuated and increased by the same process by which it was at first secured; by unceasing prayer to God, by impassioned

desires after God, by estimating it, by seeking it with tireless ardor, by deeming all else loss and failure without it. . . . Praying hearts only are the hearts filled with this holy oil; praying lips only are anointed with this divine unction. . . . Prayer, much prayer, is the price of preaching unction; prayer, much prayer, is the one, sole condition of keeping this unction.[12]

In addition to such gifts as humility, wisdom, fortitude, and special charisms for ministry, Christians need to pray for perfect wholeness understood as perfect conformity to Jesus Christ, which is, indeed, another way of describing Christian salvation. It must not be forgotten that prayer brings healing as well as meaning to our lives. As Barth puts it, "As the Christian prays, he actually anticipates his own liberation from anxiety even when engulfed by it. Praying to God, he can no longer have it, nor be possessed by it."[13] Ellul reveals that it is "prayer which restores my energies, takes away my fatigue, and which to the very end makes tranquilizers useless, for it eases every tension, every conflict."[14]

Perfect wholeness, just as perfect love, is primarily an eschatological goal, but it can be realized in part here and now. We cannot attain the absolute perfection whereby sin is transcended, but we can attain in this life a relative perfection whereby sin is surmounted through faith and love.

Social justice, too, should be a matter for Christian prayer. Yet civil righteousness, which can be realized through social reform and legislation, must never be confused with kingdom righteousness, the eschatological ideal. Civil righteousness, which is law with justice, is qualitatively different from kingdom righteousness, which is characterized by the violence of love that overcomes the adversary through self-sacrifice. We can work for and attain a measure of social justice, but kingdom righteousness is wholly a gift of God. This is not to say that the two are unrelated: kingdom righteousness is the transcendent ideal by which we can measure our progress toward an ever greater degree of social justice.

The salvation and happiness of humanity are never to pre-empt the concern to give glory to God and to uphold his truth in our words and deeds. François Fénelon, Catholic mystic of eighteenth-century France, rightly contends that "we must want the glory of God more than our own beatitude. We must only want this beatitude to add to his glory, as the thing which we want the least for the sake of the thing which we want the most."[15]

We should pray for the glory of God not only as an eschatological goal but also as a present experience in our lives. Our prayers should be that the glory of God might redound in our lives. Our hope is not only that his glory may be manifested among all peoples but that we may be glorified with him (Rom. 8:17).

Our Lord enjoins us to pray that God's will might be done on earth as it is in heaven (Matt. 6:10). This implies social righteousness as well as evangelization and humanitarian service. We should pray that the millennial promise of a transfigured earth be realized in part through greater strides toward social righteousness as well as through new breakthroughs in Christian mission.

Whenever we pray, our goal should be not to have our own way, our own comforts, our own happiness, but to serve God better. We should pray particularly for those things that contribute to our perfection in love and our conformity in Christ. We should pray for God's fullest blessings, and this means salvation, power for service and healing. It means that we should seek and pray for the presence of the Spirit even more than for his gifts. Our attention should be directed primarily to the Giver and secondarily to the gifts. Hallesby expresses my own sentiments on this point:

> If we will make use of prayer, not to wrest from God advantages for ourselves or our dear ones, or to escape from tribulations and difficulties, but to call down upon ourselves and others those things which will glorify the name of God, then we shall see the strongest and boldest promises of the Bible about prayer fulfilled also in our weak, little prayer life.[16]

## CONSTANT COMMUNION WITH GOD

Faith itself signifies a union of our wills with the will of our Redeemer, but this is a voluntaristic, not an essential union. Moreover, it is a union that must be deepened and furthered as we grow in the faith. Conversion signifies not simply the first awakening to the grace of God but continuing in this grace. It entails not only a first entrance into the kingdom of God but a constant abiding in his presence.

Paul's admonition that we should pray without ceasing (1 Thess. 5:17) points to constancy in daily prayer as well as to an attitude of prayerfulness. According to Thomas Aquinas, Paul's words refer to persistence "in the desire of the one thing needful." This kind of prayer means living in the constant awareness of the presence of God. It is reflected in Psalm 34:1 (NEB): "I will bless the Lord continually; his praise shall be always on my lips." For Charles Spurgeon, "the habit of prayer is good, but the spirit of prayer is better. Regular retirement is to be maintained, but continued communion with God is to be our aim."[17] This indeed is what Brother Lawrence meant by "the practice of the presence of God."[18]

The Christian faith is an ongoing dialectic between prayerfulness and service. Both are crucial goals in the life of prayer. It is a profound misunderstanding to contend that "helping hands are more holy than praying lips," a maxim that reflects the mentality of the Enlightenment. Service in love is made possible only because of communion with God in prayer. We cannot love our neighbor with the love of God unless and until we are united with God in faith.

Despite the tendency in a certain type of mysticism to focus attention away from the crying needs of the world to the eternal ground and depth of all being, the Christian mystics at their best perceived the organic relationship between the life of prayer and the service of our neighbor. This was not so much because of their mysticism but because their piety was shaped in part by an immersion in biblical truth.[19] Teresa of Avila confessed, "For my part, and I have been long at it, I desire no other gift of prayer than that which ends in making me a better and better woman. By its fruits your prayer will be known to yourselves and others."[20] In this kind of perspective, wounded servanthood embraces the true meaning of sanctity.

Just as prayer is integrally related to service, so it is even more closely connected with devotion. Prayer is the source and mainstay of devotion just as devotion is the culmination and fruition of prayer. According to Heiler, prayer presupposes devotion, which he understands as a solemn, consecrated mood of the soul.[21] In my understanding, devotion also entails the engagement of the soul in rendering homage to God and fulfilling those duties that pertain exclusively to God. It is possible to speak of a life of devotion that includes and is sustained by prayer.

Faith is the key to both prayer and devotion. We cannot live the Christian life apart from faith. And faith needs constantly to be cultivated and deepened. The mystics as well as the prophets saw the decisive role of faith, though sometimes the former spoke of faith as being transcended by love and the vision of God, realizable even in this life.

Brother Lawrence was one mystic who emphasized the need to walk by faith alone: "God has many ways of drawing us to Himself. He sometimes hides Himself from us; but *faith* alone, which will not fail us in time of need, ought to be our support, and the foundation of our confidence, which must be all in God."[22] John of the Cross was also acutely aware of the importance of walking only by faith, particularly in the dark night of the soul, when God's light is so overwhelming that it blinds us. From the evangelical perspective, it is more proper to speak of God withholding the blazing light of his glory from us until we are transformed in this glory in the eschatological fulfillment. To be sure, we already partake of the glory of the eschaton in faith, but this glory is yet to be revealed in all its brightness and splendor.

What is needed for a revitalized prayer life is a renewal of faith in the living Savior, Jesus Christ. Faith cannot be taken for granted. It must be fought for and recovered time and again. Faith can work wonders in the Christian life because faith places us in contact with the power of God himself. As Sibbes puts it, "Faith is an almighty grace, wrought by the power of God, and laying hold upon that power, it lays hold upon omnipotency, and therefore it can do wonders."[23] Indeed, according to Calvin faith in God is the one sure defense against the power of sin and death: "To flee unto God is the only stay which can support us in our afflictions, the only armour which renders us invincible."[24]

## PERSONAL AND SOCIAL RELIGION

The ideal, the primary goal of prophetic religion is not solitary contemplation (as in some types of mysticism) but instead the blessed fellowship, the "beloved community." Solitary prayer is still important, but it is a secondary goal. Our attention should be focused not so much on the vision of God as on the service of God. Our aim is to glorify God in the worship of him and in the service of our neighbor.

The Christian faith is not only deeply personal but also radically social. Its concern is not just with the salvation of individual souls but with the holy community. Bonhoeffer considered "life together" an apt description of Christian experience. The Christian ideal is not "holy solitaries" but "social holiness" (Wesley). According to Richard Sibbes, "it is an ill sign when any man will be a solitary Christian, and will stand alone by himself. As we are knit to Christ by faith, so we must be knit to the communion of saints by love."[25] We believe by ourselves but not for ourselves or unto ourselves. Faith cannot remain in isolation, but it actively seeks the good of others. Christian religion is personal but not individualistic; it is social but not collectivistic (where the individual is absorbed into the group).

In emphasizing the social character of Christian faith, we

must not lose sight of the truth that Christianity is a profoundly personal and individual affair as well. There is a reaction today against individualistic piety and even against private prayer. The fact remains that we enter the kingdom of God one by one. We finally have to stand alone before God and give an account of our misdeeds. Others cannot believe or repent for us. Every person has to make a solitary decision for Christ, even though he or she may well receive encouragement and direction from the community of faith. There is no such thing as a vicarious faith. We have to make the decision of faith alone just as we have to die alone. Others can pray for us, but their prayers cannot take the place of our praying.

At the same time, solitary prayer is a means to the blessed fellowship. Jesus himself often prayed alone. We read that "in the morning, a great while before day, he rose and went out to a lonely place, and there he prayed" (Mark 1:35). Yet he returned to the company of his disciples in order to resume his ministry to a fallen humanity.

The Christian life is characterized by the dialectic of withdrawal and return. As Meister Eckhart put it, "What a man takes in by contemplation, he must pour out in love." It is not detachment from the world nor escape from the world but the conversion of the world to the gospel that is the spiritual mandate of our faith.

It is customary in both Neo-Protestantism and Neo-Catholicism today to deride the otherworldly piety of a past era and to emphasize the need for identification with the oppressed of the world in their struggle for liberation. It is possible to go so far in this direction that we lose sight of the fact that meaningful identification with the oppressed rests upon a prior identification with the Savior of the oppressed. Richard Baxter's admonition has not lost its relevance:

> We are fled so far from the solitude of superstition, that we have cast off the solitude of contemplative devotion. . . . We seldom read of God's appearing by himself or his angels to any of his prophets or saints in a throng, but frequently when they are alone.[26]

We enter the kingdom one by one, but we immediately find ourselves in the company of fellow saints. Once we believe, we are upheld and supported by the whole body of Christ. The church is the "mother" of the faithful (cf. Isa. 66:8; Ps. 87:5; Gal. 4:26), the source of sustenance and inspiration. The church nurtures and equips her children for battle in the world.

The final goal of prayer is both personal salvation and the transformation of the world into the kingdom of God. God is glorified even when one sinner repents. But he is even more glorified when a new social order is established, a holy community, where peace and justice reign, where Jesus Christ is acclaimed Lord, King, and Savior.

## THE COMING OF THE KINGDOM

The kingdom will come only through great tribulation (Acts 14:22). There will be a darkness before the dawn, an agonizing struggle before the victory. Calvin put it this way: "We must endure patiently, because God will not have us come to his kingdom with, so to speak, one leap, but will have us negotiate [cross] this world through thorns and briars, so that we shall have much trouble in getting through and we shall be in great distress."[27] Yet Calvin saw the Christian life not as one of defeat but as a struggle through to victory: "It is true that our faith gets the upper hand even now, but we do not yet receive the full fruit of it, nor do we fully enjoy it. Therefore we must determine with ourselves to fight and groan continually and yet, at the same time, to rejoice also."[28]

This note of striving for the crown of victory is also present among many of the mystics as well as the Pietists and Puritans. Thomas à Kempis advised:

> Always be ready for battle if you wish for victory; you cannot win the crown of patience without a struggle; if you refuse to suffer, you refuse the crown. Therefore, if you desire the crown, fight manfully and endure patiently. Without labour, no rest is won; without battle, there can be no victory.[29]

Jonathan Edwards expressed a similar sentiment: "Without earnestness there is no getting along in that narrow way that leads to life. . . . Without earnest labor, there is no ascending the steep and high hill of Zion."[30] Jacob Boehme, too, saw that the life of prayer is not a bed of roses: "It often happens that the holiest souls become thus covered and melancholy. God often allows this to happen so that they might be tested and strive for the noble conqueror's crown."[31]

In both the Old and New Testaments, the day of the Lord is depicted as a "day of darkness," since it means the coming of judgment as well as of grace (Joel 2:1, 2; Amos 5:18–20). Forsyth aptly declared, "By terrible things in righteousness dost Thou answer us, O God of our salvation. When we pray for the kingdom to come, we know not what we ask."[32] To pray for the coming of the kingdom means to pray not for social revolution (though this may come as a result) but for spiritual invasion. It means to be willing to carry the cross, to suffer afflictions for the sake of Christ. Yet it is better to go to heaven bruised than to go to hell sound (Sibbes).

We move forward toward the goal of the heavenly Jerusalem not only in joy and hope but also in trepidation, since we know that the last judgment will precede the eternal glory. Yet we also have the assurance of ultimate victory, for we know on the basis of Holy Scripture that the war has already been won and that the powers of darkness are already defeated. We also know that those who trust in Jesus Christ for their salvation will be spared the torments of final rejection by a God who is wrathful even in his love and merciful even in his wrath. Those who are united to Jesus Christ in faith will still have to pass through the judgment, but they can be assured that the fire of God's wrath will be at the same time the purifying fire of his love which will prepare them for the crown of glory.

The believer can press on in the lively hope of his coming reward, a reward based not on his merits but on the merits of his Savior, Jesus Christ. The Christian pilgrim will be buoyed up by these words of encouragement from the apostle Paul: "May the

God of hope fill you with all joy and peace in believing, so that by the power of the Holy Spirit you may abound in hope" (Rom. 15:13).

The Christian hope gives us not only the certitude of final victory but also the assurance that we can endure and overcome in this present vale of tribulation. This note is clearly evident in Calvin's celebrated hymn "I Greet Thee, Who My Sure Redeemer Art":

> Our hope is in no other save in Thee,
>   Our faith is built upon Thy promise free;
> Come, give us peace, make us so strong and sure,
>   That we may conquerors be and ills endure.[33]

As we pray for the coming of the kingdom we pray for things beyond our comprehension, mysteries too great for reason to grasp. Luther was keenly aware of this:

> If we want to describe our prayers, they are really nothing else than the stammering of children who ask for bread or a morsel before meals. For we do not know what we should ask for. The things we ask for are beyond our comprehension, and He who bestows them is greater; and the things are also too great for our narrow hearts to be able to understand.[34]

Just as we have to walk by faith alone so we must pray on the basis of faith alone. We already possess the glory and rapture of the kingdom, but these blessings are still hidden from us. Faith itself is sometimes illumined so that we can have a foretaste of the glory that lies ahead (Rom. 8:23; 2 Cor. 1:22; Eph. 1:13, 14), but this experience should not make us complacent but instead all the more eager to lay hold of what has been promised.

The Christian can face the future with a holy optimism, knowing that Jesus Christ is the victor over all the powers of death, hell, and darkness. His reign is already in force, and it will become ever more visible to the eyes of faith as the great missionary mandate of the church is carried forward. Sibbes gives voice to this joyous confidence: "At the conversion of the Jews and the confusion of antichrist, then it will appear more and more that he is King of the world indeed. . . . There are glorious times coming, especially the glorious day of the resurrection."[35]

Prayer is the antidote to fearfulness, for it is rooted in a faith that God has overcome, that he is overcoming now, and that he will overcome. This is why we need to "strengthen the weak hands, and make firm the feeble knees." We need to say to those "who are of a fearful heart, 'Be strong, fear not! Behold, your God will come with vengeance, with the recompense of God. He will come and save you" (Isa. 35:3, 4). To pray for the coming of the kingdom is to pray for the manifestation and deepening fulfillment of the victory of Jesus Christ in the life of the church and world today as well as at the end of the age.

## NOTES

1. Richard Sibbes, *The Complete Works of Richard Sibbes*, ed. and trans. Alexander Balloch Grosart (Edinburgh: Nichol, 1862–1864), Vol. 6, p. 481.
2. See Sibbes, *Complete Works* Vol. 5, pp. 206, 491, 529. According to Sibbes, on the day of resurrection the union of grace will become a union of glory, but it will be the same union, though now intensified and deepened.
3. Leon Cristiani, *St. Bernard of Clairvaux*, trans. M. Angeline Bouchard (Boston: Daughters of St. Paul, 1977), p. 59.
4. Marvin H. Pope maintains that the descriptions of human lovers in the Song of Songs frequently allude to pagan deities. See his *Song of Songs: A New Translation with Introduction and Commentary* (Garden City, N.Y.: Doubleday, Anchor Bible Series, 1977).
5. David Bruening, ed., *The Evangelical Hymnal* (St. Louis: Eden, 1922), p. 207.
6. *Luther's Works*, Vol. 24, ed. Jaroslav Pelikan (St. Louis: Concordia, 1961), p. 399.
7. Sibbes, *Complete Works*, Vol. 1, p. 54.
8. Cited in Friedrich Heiler, *Prayer*, trans. and ed. Samuel McComb (New York: Oxford University Press, 1958), p. 132.
9. Ralph G. Turnbull, ed., *Devotions of Jonathan Edwards* (Grand Rapids, Mich.: Baker, 1959), p. 59.
10. In John E. L. Oulton and Henry Chadwick, eds., *Alexandrian Christianity* (Philadelphia: Westminster Press, n.d.), p. 219.
11. John Calvin, *Sermons on the Epistle to the Ephesians* (Edinburgh: Banner of Truth Trust, 1975), p. 269.

12. E. M. Bounds, *Power Through Prayer* (Grand Rapids, Mich.: Baker, 1979, 8th printing), p. 100.

13. Karl Barth, *Church Dogmatics,* Vol. IV, 3, b, p. 673.

14. Jacques Ellul, *Prayer and Modern Man,* trans. C. Edward Hopkin (New York: Seabury Press, 1970), p. 69.

15. François Fénelon, *Christian Perfection,* ed. Charles F. Whiston, trans. Mildred Whitney Stillman (New York: Harper, 1947), p. 139.

16. Hallesby, *Prayer,* trans. Clarence Carlsen (Minneapolis: Augsburg, 1931), p. 128.

17. Ernest W. Bacon, *Spurgeon: Heir of the Puritans* (Grand Rapids, Mich.: Eerdmans, 1968), p. 151.

18. See Nicholas Herman (Brother Lawrence), *The Practice of the Presence of God* (New York: Revell, 1958).

19. The denigration of this world was present to a greater degree among those mystics who were consistent in their mysticism, who were closer to Platonism and Neo-Platonism than to biblical thought. Neo-Platonic motifs are especially evident in Dionysius the Pseudo-Areopagite, Evagrius, John Scotus Erigena, and Angelus Silesius.

20. Cited in Olive Wyon, *The School of Prayer,* 2nd ed. (New York: Macmillan, 1966), p. 64.

21. Heiler, *Prayer,* pp. 360–363.

22. Brother Lawrence, *The Practice of the Presence of God,* p. 59.

23. Sibbes, *Complete Works,* Vol. 1, p. 366.

24. John Calvin, *Genesis,* trans. and ed. John King (Edinburgh: Banner of Truth Trust, 1975), Vol. 2, p. 302.

25. Sibbes, *Complete Works,* Vol. 3, p. 432.

26. Cited in Gordon Stevens Wakefield, *Puritan Devotion* (London: Epworth Press, 1957), p. 67.

27. Calvin, *Sermons on the Epistle to the Ephesians,* p. 77.

28. *Ibid.,* pp. 77, 78.

29. Thomas à Kempis, *The Imitation of Christ,* trans. Leo Sherley-Price (London: Penguin Classics, 1959), p. 116. (Reprint.)

30. Jonathan Edwards, *Treatise Concerning Religious Affections* in *Works of Jonathan Edwards* (New Haven, Conn.: Yale University Press 1976), Vol. 2, pp. 387, 388.

31. *Jacob Boehme—The Way to Christ,* trans. Peter Erb (New York: Paulist Press, 1978), p. 261.

32. Peter T. Forsyth, *The Justification of God* (London: Independent Press, 1948), p. 222.

33. *Psalter Hymnal* (Grand Rapids, Mich.: Board of Publications of the Christian Reformed Church, 1976), pp. 502, 503.

34. *Luther's Works,* Vol. 3, ed. J. Pelikan, p. 159.

35. Sibbes, *Complete Works,* Vol. 5, p. 490.

# Scripture Index

# Name Index

# Subject Index